GASTRIC SLEEVE BARIATRIC COOKBOOK FOR BEGINNERS:

Simple, Easy, Healthy & Delicious Recipes for Maximize Your Weight Loss (Before & After Surgery)

INTRODUCTION

First and foremost, congratulations on complepang your gastric sleeve bariatric surgery. Thank you for choosing this book, and it is my pleasure to assist you on your path.

There are many procedures. A gastric sleeve is one of the surgical procedures that help you lose weight by shrinking your stomach. Sleeve gastronomy or vertical sleeve gastronomy are two terms for the same operation. This procedure is one of the most prevalent types of bariatric surgery. Part of your stomach has permanently taked this treatment, which takes roughly 70 to 80 percent of the time. Your stomach has shrunk after these parts were taked. Ghrelin hormones are eliminated as a large portion of your stomach gut is taked during this treatment. Hunger hormones are a term for these hormones. Because these hormones aren't present, you can manage your appetite and never feel hungry. If you follow a suitable eapang plan after gastric sleeve bariatric surgery, you can lose 60 percent of your excess weight in 1 to 1.5 years. Following surgery, you will need to make specific dietary changes, such as lowering your calorie and carbohydrate intake, avoiding sugary foods, and eapang more fiber and starchy foods. Increase your consumption of protein-rich meals and beverages, as well as liquid foods.

The book includes easy-to-understand information regarding gastric sleeve bariatric surgery and post-surgical diet programs, as well as healthful and delectable bowles that are permitted after gastric sleeve surgery. These bowles are organized into four categories to correspond to the four stages of the post-surgery diet. In this book, I discovered several delicious and easy-to-make recipes, as well as delightful and nutrient-dense shakes and smoothies, as well as some beneficial soft food combos.

My objective is to offer you as much information as possible on gastric sleeve bariatric surgery and the gastric sleeve diet. The book includes detailed information about the procedure and its advantages, as well as pre-and post-surgical advice. On this subject, there are some books accessible on the market. Thank you for picking my book; I hope it will assist you in achieving your objective.

WHAT IS GASTRIC SLEEVE WEIGHT LOSS SURGERY?

Are you wondering of gastric sleeve surgery because you've tried diets and exercise for years and still can't seem to lose weight? You'll want to know the dangers and advantages, as well as what qualifies someone for the procedure and what long-term commitments you'll need to retain the outcomes.

During this procedure, doctors take a section of your stomach and add the remaining pieces together to form a fresh "sleeve" stomach the size of a banana. You'll feel full a lot faster than you did before with only a little sack (approximately 1/10th the size of your previous stomach). You won't be able to consume as much food as you used to, which will aid in weight loss. Anothermore, the procedure eliminates the region of your stomach that produces a hormone that increases your hunger.

It's Not the Same As Gastric Bypass

The surgeon makes a pany pouch that bypasses most of your stomach and goes straight to your intespane in a gastric bypass procedure.

BMIs of at least 40 make patients for gastric sleeve surgery the best candidates. This signifies you're at least 100 pounds over your desired weight. It may be a helpful alternative for certain people who are too obese for gastric bypass surgery.

What Takes Place

The operation takes around an hour to complete. Your surgeon will make a few small slits in your stomach and implant a laparoscope, which is camera-equipped equipment that delivers images to a monitor. The surgeon will next use the extra cuts to implant different medical devices and take 3/4 of your stomach. Finally, the rest of your stomach will be readded to form the "sleeve" or bowle.

You might be in the hospital for two or three days. The surgery is irreversible.

Fresh Ways of Eapang

You'll only consume clear drinks the first day following surgery. You'll be able to consume pureed foods and protein drinks by the time you leave the hospital, and you'll be able to do so for around four weeks.

Always keep in mind that you will need to modify your eapang routines going forward. After the first month, you'll gradually transition to soft solid meals. Other things to bear in mind include:

- Before swallowing, everything must be properly chewed.

- Avoid drinking when eapang to avoid overfilling your fresh stomach.
- Drink liquids within 30 minutes of finishing a meal.
- Limit your intake of high-calorie drinks and snacks.
- Take daily vitamin and mineral supplements.

You can resume regular meals after two or three months. However, keep in mind that you won't consume as much as you used to.

TABLE OF CONTENTS

1. CINNAMON AND LEMON TEA

Ready In: 8mins

Ingredients: 6

Serves: 1-2

INGREDIENTS:

- 2 bowls water
- 1/4 tsp clove
- 1/4 tsp cinnamon
- 1 tea bag (I use Lipton strong black tea)
- 1 btsp lemon juice concentrate
- 2 btbsp brown sugar

INSTRUCTIONS:

1. In a pan, add water, cinnamon, and cloves.
2. up to a boil.
3. When the required strength is reached, & a tea bag and let it soak at a lower heat. Normally, I wait two mins.
4. Add sugar and 1 tsp. of lemon juice. Depending on the concentration, more or less lemon juice may be required. Because the sort I use is rather potent, I just use a teaspoon. Depending on your liking, use less sugar or a replacement.
5. Pour into bowls after heating in a pan. For an iced tea, cool and serve with ice.

NUTRITION INFO:

Serving Size: 1 (254) g Servings Per Recipe: 1

Calories: 108.4 Calories to Fat 1 g Total Fat 0.1 g Saturated Fat 0 g Cholesterol 0 mg Sodium 22.8 mg Total Carbohydrate 28 g

2. TURMERIC TEA

PREP TIME: 5 mins

COOK TIME: 15 mins

TOTAL TIME: 20 mins

SERVINGS: 2 servings

INGREDIENTS:

- 1/2 tsp ground turmeric
- 1/4 tsp black pepper
- 2 tbsp lemon juice
- 2 bowls water
- 2 tsp raw honey

INSTRUCTIONS:

1. Add water, turmeric, lemon juice, & black pepper to a small saucepan. Heat while whisking the ingredients together. Once it just starts to boil, reduce the heat to low & let the tea boil for 10 mins.
2. After the tea has completed simmering, remove it from the heat, stir in the honey, and let it sit for a few seconds to cool.
3. To remove the black pepper, drain the tea into a cup before sipping.

CALORIES: 27kcal, CARBOHYDRATES: 7g, PROTEIN: 1g, FAT: 1g, SODIUM: 13mg, SUGAR: 6g, SATURATED FAT: 1g, VITAMIN C: 6mg, CALCIUM: 7mg, IRON: 1mg

3. BASIL TEA

Prep Time: 5 minutes

Cook Time: 0 minutes

Yield: 1 drink

Ingredients:

- 1 bag black tea
- 6 large leaves basil
- 1/2 lemon slice

Instructions:

1. Water is brought to a boil.
2. Basil leaves and a lemon circle should be lightly muddled (mashed) in the bottom of a tea glass using a wooden spoon.
3. To the mug, add the black tea bag. After adding the water, steep for five minutes. Drink the basil, lemon, and tea bag right away.

4. STRAWBERRY, LIME, CUCUMBER, AND MINT INFUSED WATER

Yield: 2 QUARTS

Prep time: 5 MINUTES

Additional time: 10 MINUTES

Total time: 15 MINUTES

Ingredients:

- 1 bowl sliced strawberries
- 1 bowl sliced cucumbers
- 2 limes, sliced
- 1/4 bowl fresh mint leaves
- Ice cubes
- Water

Instructions:

1. Layer the strawberries, cucumbers, lime slices, & mint leaves with the ice cubes in a half-gallon container or a 2-quart pitcher. Add water to the container or pitcher. Enjoy after 10 mins of chilling.

Notes:

I could get 2- 4 fill-ups from a batch of flavorings, however you might want to switch to a stronger flavoring more quickly.

Use sparkling water in place of still water if you choose.

Naturally, the flavor will be greater the longer the water rests. It starts off moderate, but grows stronger over time (or overnight).

Nutrition Information:

YIELD: 8 SERVING SIZE: 1 bowl

Amount Per Serving: CALORIES: 14TOTAL FAT: 0gSATURATED FAT: 0gTRANS FAT: 0gUNSATURATED FAT: 0gCHOLESTEROL: 0mgSODIUM: 2mgCARBOHYDRATES: 4gFIBER: 1gSUGAR: 2gPROTEIN: 0g

5. MINI ORANGE INFUSED WATER

PREP TIME: 5 mins

TOTAL TIME: 5 mins

SERVINGS: 8

INGREDIENTS:

- 8 bowls filtered water (2 liters)
- 1 orange , sliced
- 1/2 tsp vanilla remove (optional)

INSTRUCTIONS:

1. Slice the orange into slices that are about a quarter-inch thick, then pour 8 cups of water into a pitcher. Depending on how big your pitcher's mouth is, cut them in half or quarters. (You want them to be simple to remove for cleaning afterwards.)
2. Before serving, whisk the water thoroughly before adding the orange segments and vanilla, and then allow the flavors blend for 2 to 4 hours in the

refrigerator. Any leftovers should be kept in the freeze for up to three days before serving.

NOTES:

The dietary data only applies to one of eight bowls. This is determined automatically, but it's only an estimate and not a promise.

NUTRITION:

Calories: 8kcal, Carbohydrates: 1g, Sodium: 12mg, Potassium: 29mg, Sugar: 1g, Vitamin A: 35IU, Vitamin C: 8.7mg, Calcium: 14mg

6. WATERMELON MINT INFUSED WATER

Yield: 2

Prep time: 8 HOURS

Total time: 8 HOURS

Ingredients:

- 1 16 oz. canning container
- ½ bowl fresh watermelon cut into chunks
- ¼ of fresh mint leaves

Instructions:

1. Use a spoon or fork to slightly crush the watermelon pieces and fresh mint leaves in the container to release the juices (ripping the leaves will also infuse your water even more).
2. For the greatest flavor, add water to the jar, cover it, and put it in the refrigerator overnight.

Notes:

1 16 oz. container = 2 servings.

Simply double or cut the components in half and chill overnight if you'd like to use a bigger or smaller canning jar.

Nutrition Information:

YIELD: 2 SERVING SIZE: 1

Amount Per Serving: CALORIES: 12TOTAL FAT: 0gSATURATED FAT: 0gTRANS FAT: 0gUNSATURATED FAT: 0gCHOLESTEROL: 0mgSODIUM: 1mgCARBOHYDRATES: 3gFIBER: 0gSUGAR: 2gPROTEIN: 0g

7. STRAWBERRY MINT INFUSED WATER

Prep Time: 5 minutes

Total Time: 5 minutes

Servings: 8 servings

Calories: 6kcal

Ingredients:

- 12 strawberries, sliced
- ¼ bowl mint leaves
- ½ gallon filtered water

Instructions:

1. A half-gallon pitcher should include strawberries & mint leaves in the bottom.
2. Place purified water inside.

3. Before consuming, stir, cover, and store in refrigerator for at least 3 to 4 hours.
4. At the close of the day, replenish the container with additional filtered water. Before needing to create fresh, you can do this for two to three days.

Nutrition:

Calories: 6kcal | Carbohydrates: 1g | Sodium: 12mg | Potassium: 35mg | Vitamin A: 60IU | Vitamin C: 11.1mg | Calcium: 13mg | Iron: 0.1mg

8. LEMON MELON POPSICLE

Prep Time: 15 minutes

Additional Time: 6 hours

Total Time: 6 hours 15 minutes

Servings: 10 popsicles

Ingredients:

- 5 ½ bowls watermelon chop into squares before measuring
- ⅓ bowl freshly squeezed lemon juice about 2 large lemons or 3 small lemons juiced
- 1 tbsp lemon zest zest of 1 large lemon / 2 small
- 18 fresh mint leaves stems taked, about 4 sprigs

Instructions:

1. Lemons are zested and juiced, and watermelon is cut. In a blender, blend the watermelon, lemon juice, lemon zest, & mint leaves; process until smooth.

2. Fill each popsicle mold with the watermelon popsicle mixture, leaving 1 inch of room at the top of each mold. Add the popsicle sticks next. Once frozen thoroughly, place the mold in the freezer for 6–12 hours.
3. Bring the mold to the freezer, then use a butter knife to gently scrape the mold's edges to release the popsicles. Once the popsicles have been removed, consume them right away since they will quickly melt. Enjoy!

Notes:

1. Popsicles left over can be kept in the freezer for two months in a tight container sandwiched between parchment paper. To avoid freezer burn, make sure the popsicles are not touching and that the container has parchment paper on the top and bottom.
2. The popsicle mixture can be sweetened by adding 2 Tbsp- 14 bowl honey or agave if the watermelon isn't particularly sweet.
3. Lemon juice can be substituted for lime juice 1:1, however lime zest needs to be reduced by half (12 Tbsp as opposed to 1).

Nutrition:

Serving: 1popsicle | Calories: 28kcal | Carbohydrates: 7g | Protein: 1g | Saturated Fat: 1g | Polyunsaturated Fat: 1g | Monounsaturated Fat: 1g | Sodium: 2mg | Potassium: 113mg | Fiber: 1g | Sugar: 5g | Vitamin A: 553IU | Fat: 1g | Vitamin C: 11mg | Calcium: 12mg | Iron: 1mg

9. RESPBERRY POPSICLE

Prep Time: 5 mins

Cook Time: 0 mins

Freezing time: 4 hrs

Equipment:

Popsicle sticks & molds

Food processor or stick/immersion blender

Ingredients:

- 4 bowls (1.1 lbs/ 500gms) fresh or frozen raspberries
- ½ tbsp freshly squeezed lime juice
- ¼ bowl maple syrup

Instructions:

1. Allow the raspberries to thaw if using frozen ones. If using fresh, ensure sure all the berries are in good condition before using.
2. Juice the lime after slicing it in half.
3. Put the raspberries in a deep container that you may use as a food processor or an immersion/stick blender.
4. After adding, thoroughly blend in the lime juice & maple syrup until smooth.
5. Pour mixture into molds for popsicles, insert sticks, and freeze for at at least four hours or till solid.
6. Take to the molds to serve and enjoy!

10. REFRESHING STRAWBERRY LIMEADE

SERVINGS: 6 servings

PREP TIME: 10 mins

COOK TIME: 0 mins

TOTAL TIME: 10 mins

Ingredients:

- 4 bowls fresh strawberries hulled
- 12 large mint leaves
- 1/2 bowl agave nectar
- 1/2 bowl fresh lime juice
- 6 bowls cold water
- ice
- more strawberries for garnishing
- mint for garnishing

Instructions:

1. Put strawberries & mint leaves in a pitcher's base. Make a paste out of them by mashing and squishing them together with a wooden spoon or another item. Additionally, "you may blitz in a food processor."
2. Add agave, lime juice, and cold water. Stir well. Taste and make adjustments as desired. Add extra strawberries and mint for garnish after pouring over ice.

Nutrition:

Calories: 94kcal | Carbohydrates: 23g | Protein: 1g | Saturated Fat: 1g | Sodium: 15mg | Potassium: 182mg | Fiber: 2g | Sugar: 18g | Vitamin A: 107IU | Fat: 1g | Vitamin C: 63mg | Calcium: 30mg | Iron: 1mg

CHAPTER 2

FULL LIQUIDS

11. CHOCOLATE PEANUT BUTTER SHAKE

Prep/Total Time: 10 min.

Makes: 2 servings

Ingredients:

- 3/4 bowl 2% milk
- 1-1/2 bowls chocolate ice cream
- 1/4 bowl creamy peanut butter
- 2 tbsp chocolate syrup
- Sweetened whipped cream, cut-up tiny peanut butter cups, and more chocolate syrup are all optional additions.

Instructions:

1. Mix the milk, ice cream, peanut butter, and syrup in a blender; then, with the lid on, blend until smooth. Add

whipped cream, peanut butter cups, and more chocolate syrup as garnish, if desired.

Nutrition Facts:

1 bowl: 501 calories, 29g fat (11g saturated fat), 41mg cholesterol, 51g carbohydrate (43g sugars, 3g fiber), 262mg sodium, 14g protein.

12. PEVERY BLUEBERRY PROTEIN SHAKE

Prep Time: 5 MINS

Cook Time: 0 MINS

Total Time: 5 MINS

Servings (adjustable): 1

Calories: 180

Ingredients:

- ⅓ bowl cottage cheese (non-fat for Simply Filling; I prefer full fat)
- 2 tbsp (15.5 g) vanilla protein powder (I used Vanilla TrimShake to doTERRA)
- ¼ bowl blueberries
- ½ bowl frozen pevery slices
- ¼ bowl water
- 8-12 ice cubes
- Sweetener as need (I used 2 packets of Truvia)

Instructions:

1. Blend everything together in a powerful blender until it is smooth and creamy.

Notes:

If you count the fruit...

Weight Watchers Points+: 4

Weight Watchers SmartPoints: 6

If you don't count the fruit: 134 calories, 3.0 g fat, 9.2 g carbs, 2.5 g fiber, 18.4 g protein, 3 Weight Watchers Points+, 4 WW Freestyle SmartPoints.

Nutrition Facts:

Amount Per Serving (1 smoothie)

Calories 180Calories to Fat 28 Fat 3.1g5% Carbohydrates 21g7% Fiber 4.4g18% Protein 18.6g

13. CHOCOLATE MILKSHAKE

Prep: 10 Min

Total: 10 Min

Servings: 2

Ingredients:

- ¾ bowl milk
- ¼ bowl chocolate-flavored syrup
- 3 scoops (1/2 bowl every) vanilla ice cream

Steps:

1. Place milk & syrup in a blender. For two seconds, cover and combine at high speed.
2. Include ice cream. Cover and combine for approximately 5 seconds on low speed, or until smooth. Add liquid to glasses. Serve right away.

Tips:

1. Don't forget to add maraschino cherries, sprinkles, or a creamy topping. Find genuine cream-based chilled whipped topping in a can, and for fun, look for biodegradable paper straws or long heatdae spoons.
2. Put together a milkshake station for the family to use the recipe as a guide (have double the ingredients available). Toppings for the milkshakes can include little bowls of candy-coated chocolate pieces, thick butterscotch or caramel ice cream topping, toffee baking bits, broken cream-filled wafer cookies, or gingersnaps. Use a powerful blender, please!
3. The thick shakes will have a '50s diner feel if 1 tbsp of malted milk powder is added.

Nutrition:

380 Calories, 14g Total Fat, 55g Total Carbohydrate, 8g Protein, 41g Sugars

14. APPLE PEANUT BUTTER SHAKE

Active: 5 mins

Total: 5 mins

Servings: 1

Ingredients:

- 1 bowl unsweetened almond milk
- 1 small apple, chopped
- 2 tbsp natural peanut butter
- 2 tsp honey (Optional)
- 1 tsp vanilla remove
- ¼ tsp ground cinnamon
- 4-6 ice cubes

Instructions:

Blend together ice cubes, almond milk, apple, peanut butter, honey (if using), vanilla, & cinnamon. until smooth, puree.

Equipment:

Blender

Nutrition Facts:

Serving Size: 2 1/2 bowls

Per Serving: 317 calories; protein 8.4g; carbohydrates 24.9g; dietary fiber 5.1g; sugars 14.9g; fat 18.7g; saturated fat 2.5g; vitamin a iu 522.1IU; vitamin c 5.3mg; calcium 466.1mg; iron 0.9mg; magnesium 7mg; potassium 163.7mg; sodium 278m

15. ALMOND BUTTER & BANANA PROTEIN SMOOTHIE

Total: 5 mins

Servings: 1

Ingredients:

- 1 small frozen banana
- 1 bowl unsweetened almond milk

- 2 tbsp almond butter
- 2 tbsp unflavored protein powder
- 1 tbsp sweetener of your choice (optional)
- ½ tsp ground cinnamon
- 4-6 ice cubes

Instructions:

1. Mix all ingredients together in a blender until completely smooth.

Nutrition Facts:

Serving Size: 1 3/4 bowls

Per Serving: 402 calories; protein 19.4g; carbohydrates 37.4g; dietary fiber 8.5g; sugars 14.4g; fat 21.8g; saturated fat 2.3g; vitamin a iu 568.8IU; vitamin c 8.8mg; folate 37.2mcg; calcium 410.9mg; iron 10.1mg; magnesium 140.4mg; potassium 867.1mg; sodium 375.7mg; thiamin 1.3mg.

16. CHOCOLATE ALMOND BUTTER BOWL PROTEIN SMOOTHIE

Prep Time: 5 mins

Total Time: 5 mins

Calories: 200kcal

Ingredients:

- 1 scoop chocolate protein powder this is the one I used
- 1 tbsp almond butter
- 1 tbsp unsweetened cocoa powder

- 1/2 frozen banana
- Handful of greens I like baby turnach
- 1 bowl almond milk
- dash of cinnamon

Instructions:

1. Mix everything till smooth in your blender, then enjoy!

Nutrition:

Serving: 1g | Calories: 200kcal | Carbohydrates: 21g | Protein: 7g | Fat: 13g | Saturated Fat: 1g | Cholesterol: 1mg | Sodium: 332mg | Potassium: 415mg | Fiber: 6g | Sugar: 8g | Vitamin A: 38IU | Vitamin C: 5mg | Calcium: 372mg | Iron: 1mg

17. CHOCOLATE BERRY SMOOTHIE

Prep Time: 5 mins

Cook Time: 0 mins

Total Time: 5 minutes

Yield: 2 servings

Ingredients:

- 1 bowl milk
- 1 bowl frozen berries
- 1/2 bowl frozen bananas
- 2 tbsp unsweetened cocoa powder*
- 1/2 tsp vanilla
- Stevia places, as needed

Instructions:

1. In a blender, mix the milk, berries, bananas, chocolate powder, and vanilla.
2. until creamy, process.
3. If necessary, give it a taste and add more stevia.

Notes:

1. If too much cocoa powder is used, the dish may become quite bitter. You may reduce the amount of cocoa powder to 1 tbsp if you like more sweetness than bitterness.
2. Information on nutrition is only given as a rough approximation. The numbers may fluctuate due to different brands and products. Any dietary advice should only be used as a broad guide.

Nutrition:

Serving Size: about 10 ozCalories: 138Sugar: 12 gSodium: 67 mgFat: 3 gSaturated Fat: 3 gUnsaturated Fat: 0 gTrans Fat: 0 gCarbohydrates: 24 gFiber: 4 gProtein: 6 gCholesterol: 10 mg

18. VANILLA STRAWBERRY MILKSHAKE

YIELD: 1 SERVING

PREP TIME: 8 MIN

COOK TIME: 0 MIN

INGREDIENTS:

- 1 1/2 bowls fresh ripe strawberries, hulled and sliced
- 1 tsp vanilla remove
- 2 packed bowls French vanilla bean ice cream
- 3/4 bowl coconut milk (or any milk you like)

- Optional toppings: shredded unsweetened coconut

INSTRUCTIONS:

1. Making a vanilla strawberry milkshake involves: Refresh a glass. Wash and dry the strawberries with a towel. Strawberries should be sliced and stemmed to fill one and a half dishes.
2. Freshly sliced strawberries, 1 teaspoon vanilla extract, 2 bowls of French vanilla bean ice cream, and 3/4 bowl coconut milk should all be combined in a blender. Until smooth, blend.
3. Place a strawberry or any other desired garnish on top of the vanilla strawberry milkshake after pouring it into the chilled glass you made in step 1. We enjoy including some coconut shreds. Enjoy!

Nutrition:

Energy 592.38 cal Fat40.98 g Protein7.89 g Carbs50.59 gSaturated Fat31.73 gPolyunsat Fat1.19 g

19. ALMOND RASPBERRY SMOOTHIE

Prep Time: 3 mins

Total Time: 3 mins

Servings: 2 (13 ounces/390 ml)

Calories: 307

Ingredients:

- 1.5 bowls frozen raspberries (180 grams), see note 1
- 1 bowl almond milk
- 3 tbsp almond butter , see note 2

- 3 tbsp maple syrup , see note 3
- 5 almonds , chopped (optional)

Instructions:

1. Mix raspberries, almond milk, almond butter, and maple syrup until completely smooth in a blender. If desired, taste and add extra sweetness.
2. If desired, garnish with raspberries & chopped almonds before serving!

Notes:

1. Make this smoothie thicker by using two bowls (220 grams) of raspberries.
2. Remember that almond butters come in different flavors and sweetness levels depending on the brand. I used pure butter with fewer than 5 grams of added sugar (per 100-grams). Some might have up to 40 grams. You might need to use less maple syrup as a result.
3. Any type of sweetener is acceptable. Just keep in mind that the amount used will vary depending on each person's preferences as well as how sweet the raspberries & almond butter are.
4. This recipe is simple to double.
5. Smoothies taste best when consumed immediately, but if necessary, you may preserve them in the refrigerator for up to a day.

Nutrition:

Fat17g Saturated Fat1g Sodium168mg Potassium401mg Carbohydrates37g Fiber9g Sugar23g Protein 7g

20. COCONUT STRAWBERRY PROTEIN SMOOTHIE

YIELD: 1 shake

PREP TIME: 5 mins

TOTAL TIME: 5 mins

Ingredients:

- 1 scoop strawberry protein powder
- 1 bowl strawberries fresh or frozen
- 1/2 banana frozen
- 8 oz unsweetened coconut milk
- 1/4 bowl coconut flakes

Instructions:

1. Blend the protein powder, strawberries, banana, & coconut milk on high speed until thoroughly combined. If the smoothies is too thick for your preferences, add more water while blending.
2. Add the flakes coconut and process on high until completely combined, about 15 seconds.
3. If preferred, top the dish with additional flaked coconut before serving.

Equipment:

Protein Powder

Ninja Kitchen System

CHAPTER 3

SOFT FOODS RECIPES

21. DELICIOUS PUREED CHICKEN

PREP TIME: 5 minutes

COOK TIME: 20 minutes

TOTAL TIME: 25 minutes

SERVES:4

EQUIPMENT:

High Speed Blender or Food Processor

INGREDIENTS:

- ½ tbsp Olive Oil
- ½ small Onion ,finely chopped
- 160g (1 bowl chopped) Boneless Skinless Chicken Breast or Thighs ,chopped into approx. 2.5 – 3cm (1 inch) cubes
- 300g / 11oz (2 bowls chopped) Sweet Potato ,peeled and chopped into approx. 1-1.5cm (½ inch) cubes
- 80g / ⅓ bowl Carrot peeled and chopped into approx. 1- 1.5 cm (½ inch) cubes
- 250ml / 1 bowl Chicken Stock homemade or baby friendly

INSTRUCTIONS:

1. In a medium-sized saucepan on a medium heat, heat the oil. Add the onion, and cook for two to three minutes.
2. Sauté the chicken for about 30 seconds, or until it turns opaque.
3. Sweet potato, carrot, and stock are added. For 15 mins or until the veggies are tender when forked, bring to a boil, cover, and simmer gently.
4. Transfer the chicken and veggies to a food processor or blender with a slotted spoon, reserving the cooking liquid. until desired consistency is reached. To assist obtain a thinner, smoother texture, stir in a tablespoon of the boiling broth.

NOTES:

- Chicken stock or broth enhances flavor but most of it has too much salt for infants. You can find reduced sodium stocks or stock cubes or prepare your own baby-friendly chicken stock. You might alternatively dilute the stock or just use water in its stead.

Nutrition:

Polyunsaturated Fat 1g Monounsaturated Fat 1g Sodium 59mg 2% Potassium 339mg 10% Carbohydrates 18g 6% Fiber 3g 12% Sugar 4g 4% Protein 2g 4% Vitamin A 13982IU 280% Vitamin C 4mg

22. PINTO TACO BEANS

Servings: 50 servings

Ingredients:

- Beans, pinto, canned, drained 18¾ pounds
- Onions, raw, chopped
- (2 bowls, 1 tbsp)
- 2.063 bowls
- Garlic powder ¼ bowl
- Oregano leaves, dried, ground 2 tbsp
- Pepper, black, ground 1½ tbsp
- Tomato paste, canned, without salt added
- (2 bowls, 1 tbsp) 2.063 bowls
- Water ⅓ gallon
- Chili powder 2 tbsp
- Cumin, ground 2 tbsp
- Paprika 2 tbsp
- Onion powder 2 tbsp

Instructions:

1. Drain and rinse the beans in the can.
2. Beans should be processed in a food processor until they are smooth.
3. To a food processor, add the onions, garlic, tomato paste, water, & spices. Blend well.
4. Bring ingredients to a boil in a big saucepan. Simmer for 25–30 minutes, stirring occasionally, over low heat. Serve hot.
5. Serve heated at 135°F or higher; hold for serving.

Notes:

Credipang: 2 ounce Meal/Meal Alternate

Nutrition Facts per Serving (2ounces):

Calories: 212.8 kcal | Fat: 1.8 g | Saturated fat: 0.3 g | Sodium: 429 mg | Carbohydrates: 38.5 g | Fiber: 10.4 g | Sugar: 1.3 g | Protein: 12.8 g

23. PUREED TUNA

Prep Time: 5 mins

Total Time: 5 mins

Servings: 4 ¼ bowl

Calories: 78 kcal

INGREDIENTS:

- 1 6 oz. can tuna packed in water
- 2 tsp relish
- 1-2 tbsp low-fat mayonnaise
- 2 tbsp plain Greek or Icelandic Yogurt I used Siggi's
- Salt and pepper as need if desired

INSTRUCTIONS:

1. Mix the relish and tuna pieces in a small food processor.
2. Tuna should be pulsed until the flesh is shreds.
3. Put the combined tuna and relish in a mixing basin.
4. Mix the tuna mixture with the mayonnaise and yogurt.
5. Combine everything well.
6. Add salt and pepper to taste, if desired.

7. Serve in parts of 14 bowl (2 oz).

NUTRITION:

Serving: 1/4 bowl Calories: 78kcal Carbohydrates: 1.7g
Protein: 10.5g Fat: 2.9g Saturated Fat: 0.6g Polyunsaturated
Fat: 2.1g Trans Fat: 0g Cholesterol: 19.3mg Sodium: 104.9mg
Fiber: 0g Sugar: 1.1g

24. HEALTHY SALMON PATE

Prep Time: 2 minutes

Total Time: 2 minutes

Servings: 8

servings Calories: 111kcal

Ingredients:

- 200 g cooked salmon
- 200 g cream cheese
- 0.5 lemon - juice only
- 5 g fresh dill - chopped
- 1 pinch sea salt and black pepper

Instructions:

1. Each component should be placed in a mixing basin.
2. Make sure to thoroughly combine everything.

Notes:

- To add more flavor, you might combine cooked
  salmon fillet with smoked salmon. Use less salt if
  you're using smoked salmon.

- Use a garlic & herb cream cheese if you wanted to add some garlic & herbs to this.
- Use half Greek yogurt and half cream cheese to make this dish lighter.
- A dash of smoked paprika will provide some smokey flavor.
- Red onion that has been finely sliced and stirred in will add more crunch.
- Use a vegan cream cheese to make recipe dairy-free.

Nutritional Information:

Serving: 1portion | Calories: 111kcal | Carbohydrates: 2g | Protein: 7g | Fat: 9g | Saturated Fat: 5g | Polyunsaturated Fat: 1g | Monounsaturated Fat: 3g | Cholesterol: 41mg | Sodium: 92mg | Potassium: 171mg | Fiber: 1g | Sugar: 1g | Vitamin A: 395IU | Vitamin C: 4mg | Calcium: 31mg | Iron: 1mg

25. THICK AND CREAMY MASHED BUTTERNUT SQUASH

Prep Time: 10 mins

Cook Time: 15 mins

Total Time: 25 mins

Servings: 4 servings

Calories: 171kcal

INGREDIENTS:

- 1 lb. diced and peeled raw butternut squash
- 4 tbsp unsalted butter softened

- ¼ bowl grated Parmesan cheese (not coarsely shredded)
- 1 tsp minced fresh garlic
- 1 tsp Diamond Crystal kosher salt (or ½ tsp fine salt)

INSTRUCTIONS:

1. Put the butternut squash cubes in a large dish that can go in the microwave. Add a half-bowl of water, cover, & microwave for 15 minutes or until tender. Water well.
2. In your food processor, combine the cooked butternut squash with the additional ingredients.
3. *
4. Process for 1-2 minutes, stopping occasionally to scrape the sides with a spatula until smooth. Process at first on low, then increase to high until smooth.
5. Give the mash a quick serving. For 3–4 days, store leftovers covered in the refrigerator.

NOTES:

- If using frozen butternut squash cubes, thaw them in the microwave as directed on the package and drain thoroughly.
- The easiest technique is to use a food processor. But if you don't mind a little elbow grease and a somewhat lumpier consistency, you may use a potato masher/even a fork.

NUTRITION PER SERVING:

Serving: 0.25recipe | Calories: 171kcal | Carbohydrates: 12g | Protein: 3g | Fat: 13g | Saturated Fat: 8g | Sodium: 380mg | Fiber: 3g

26. CREAMY CARROT MASH

Prep: 10 mins

Total: 40 mins

Servings: 4

Ingredients:

- 2 pounds carrots, cut into 2-inch lengths
- Coarse salt and ground pepper
- 1 tbsp butter
- 1/4 bowl reduced-fat sour cream

Instructions:

1. Carrots should be put in a big pan. Add salt and cover with water to a depth of 1 inch. High heat, bring to a boil; lower heat to a simmer. Cook for 25 to 30 minutes, or until carrots are really tender.
2. Transfer the drained liquid to a food processor. Salt and pepper to taste; then incorporate butter & sour cream. Process for about three mins, or until smooth, scraping down the sides of the machine as needed. Serve.

27. HEALTHY CARROT MASH

SERVINGS: 4

PREP TIME: 5 MINS

COOK TIME: 20 MINS

TOTAL TIME: 25 MINS

Ingredients:

- 2 pounds carrots, about 12 large carrots, scrubbed
- 4 tbsp butter, or more as need (substitute Earth Balance for vegan)
- 1/2 bowl chicken stock, substitute vegetable stock for vegan
- salt and pepper as need
- 2 tsp garlic powder, optional

Instructions:

1. Bring water in a big saucepan to a boil.
2. Cut the carrots into uniform pieces that are about 1" in size. Boil the carrots in the water for 15- 20 minutes, or till a knife inserted into them yields a soft response. Refill the saucepan with water after draining the carrots. Butter, chicken stock, salt, pepper, & garlic powder should all be added. Using a hand masher, thoroughly blend the carrots. Purée the carrots in a food processor or immersion blender until extremely smooth. If they need additional salt or butter, taste them. Serve hot.

NUTRITION:

Calories: 170, Total Carbs: 14.5g, Protein: 2.3g, Fat: 12.2g, Fiber: 3.7g, Net Carbs: 11g

28. BROCCOLI CAULIFLOWER MASH

Servings: 8

Ingredients:

- 3 tbsp extra-virgin olive oil
- 1 large head cauliflower, cut into 3/4-inch chunks
- 1 small bunch broccoli, trimmed and cut into 3/4-inch florets
- 1 tsp coarse salt
- Pepper

Instructions:

Oil in a big pot is heated up over medium-high heat. Add salt, broccoli, and cauliflower. Cook under a cover for approximately 8 minutes, stirring periodically, until partly soft. Over medium-high heat, add 3/4 bowl of water, cover, & simmer for approximately 5 mins, or until tender and most of the water has evaporated. Use a potato masher to mash. Use pepper to season.

29. CREAMY TOMATO SOUP

ACTIVE TIME:30 minutes

TOTAL TIME: 1 1/4 hours

Servings: 8

Ingredients:

- ¼ bowl (½ stick) unsalted butter
- 10 sprigs thyme, tied together

- 1 medium onion, thinly sliced
- 2 garlic cloves, thinly sliced
- ¼ bowl tomato paste
- 2 28-oz. cans whole tomatoes
- 1–2 tsp sugar, divided
- ¼ bowl (or more) heavy cream
- Kosher salt and freshly ground black pepper

Instructions:

1. Melt the butter in a large, heavy pot over medium heat. Tuck in some thyme, onion, & garlic. Cook for 10-12 mins, or until onion is totally tender and transparent. Medium-high heat is increased and tomato paste is added. Cook the paste, often stirring, for another 5 to 6 minutes, or until it starts to turn slightly caramelized.
2. To a saucepan, add tomatoes with juices, 1 teaspoon of sugar, and 8 bowls of water. Turn up the heat to high and simmer. heat to a medium setting. Simmer for 45–55 minutes, or until the flavors combine and the soup is reduced to about 2 quarts (8 bowls). Heat the soup; let it to slightly cool. Throw away thyme sprigs. Soup should be blended in tiny amounts until smooth. Back to the pot Prepare the soup two days in advance. Cover and chill after allowing to cool somewhat. Before continuing, rewarm.
3. 1/4 bowl of cream should be stirred in. Simmer soup for a further 10-15 minutes to let flavors blend. Add more salt, pepper, and 1 teaspoon of sugar as desired. If desired, add extra cream.

Nutrition Per Serving:

1 serving contains:

Calories (kcal) 150 Fat (g) 8 Saturated Fat (g) 5 Cholesterol (mg) 25 Carbohydrates (g) 17 Dietary Fiber (g) 4 Total Sugars (g) 11 Protein (g) 3 Sodium (mg) 650

30. HEALTHY TURNACH SOUP

Prep Time: 15 mins

Cook Time: 15 mins

Total Time: 30 mins

Servings: 2

Ingredients:

- 2 bowls chopped turnach (palak)
- ¼ bowl chopped onions
- ¼ tsp chopped garlic or 2 to 3 small to medium-sized garlic cloves
- 1 tbsp gram flour or chickpea flour – swap with cornmeal or all-purpose flour
- ¼ tsp ground cumin (cumin powder)
- 1 bay leaf – small sized, swap with tej patta (Indian bay leaf)
- 2 bowls water or vegetable stock
- 1 or 1.5 tbsp olive oil or butter
- ¼ tsp ground black pepper or add as required
- salt as required
- 2 to 3 tbsp coconut cream for topping, optional
- 2 to 3 pinches of crushed black pepper – optional

Instructions:

Preparation

- The turnip leaves should first be thoroughly rinsed in water several times. Finally, drain all of the water.
- Turnip leaves should be chopped and set aside. You may utilize them as well if the stems are supple.

Sautéing And Cooking Turnach Soup Mixture

- In a sauce pan, warm the oil. Sauté the bay leaf for a further 1-2 seconds.
- Garlic should now be added and sautéed until it turns light brown or browned. Garlic shouldn't be burned.
- Cook the garlic slowly over low heat. Add the chopped onions and cook until they are tender.
- Turnip, chopped, is added. Salt and black pepper are added after stirring.
- Add the gram flour or besan now. Mix thoroughly.
- Add two cups of water, then stir again.
- After bringing the mixture to a boil, simmer it for three to four minutes.
- Stir in the ground cumin well.
- Put the soup mixture on low heat for a while to allow it cool.

Making Turnach Soup

- As soon as the heat has dropped or the soup has warmed up, puree the soup mixture with a hand mixer, in a food processor, or in a blender.
- During the mixing, remove the bay leaf.
- Verify the spices and, if necessary, add more salt or pepper.

- If the soup appears thick, whisk in approximately a quarter bowl of water.
- Reheat the well blended soup for 2 to 3 minutes of simmering.
- Serve the turnip soup hot, garnished with coconut cream and freshly ground black pepper.

Notes:

Use tender, new turnip. You may also use frozen or baby turnip. Thaw the leaves of frozen turnip first. Press & squeeze all of the water into the leaves when they have thawed.

You can utilize them if the stems are tender. However, if they are stringy or fibrous, cut off the stems and utilize the leaves only.

Any neutral taspang oil, including olive oil, may be used for the oil. Butter may be added to turnip soup to make it vegetarian.

This soup is thin and light. You must incorporate some kind of starch into the soup to thicken it. 14 to 3 bowls worth of chopped potatoes should be added to the soup mixture. Add water and potatoes first. Cook potatoes till nearly done. When the turnip leaves are wilted, add them next and continue simmering. You may also add some carrots to the soup, but the soup will taste sweeter when you do.

There are two servings in this recipe. However, it is simple to scale up to produce a large quantity.

In the fridge, the soup keeps well for one to two days. Without the coconut cream, you may freeze for a few weeks as well.

With this palak soup, bread croutons work well as a garnish.

Nutrition Info:

Saturated Fat 7g Polyunsaturated Fat 2g Monounsaturated Fat 13g Sodium 622mg2 Potassium 300mg Carbohydrates 7g Fiber 2g Sugar 1g Protein 3g Vitamin A 2828IU5 Vitamin B1 (Thiamine) 1mg6 Vitamin B2 (Riboflavin) 1mg5 Vitamin B3 (Niacin) 1mg Vitamin B6 1mg Vitamin C 10mg Vitamin E 3mg Vitamin K 158µg1 Calcium 54mg Vitamin B9 (Folate) 82µg Iron 2mg Magnesium 42mg Phosphorus 55mg Zinc 1mg

31. EGG SALAD

Prep time: 10 minutes

Cook time: 10 minutes

Total time:20 minutes

Servings: 4 servings

Ingredients:

- 8 eggs hard boiled and cooled
- ½ bowl mayonnaise
- 1 ½ tsp yellow mustard
- 1 green onion thinly sliced
- 1 rib celery finely diced
- 2 tsp fresh dill chopped

Instructions:

1. Divide an egg in half. Chop whites and take the yolks.
2. Till smooth and creamy, combine yolks with mayonnaise, mustard, and salt and pepper as desired.
3. Stir thoroughly after adding the other ingredients.
4. Serve over lettuce or on toast.

Nutrition information:

Calories: 320 | Carbohydrates: 1g | Protein: 11g | Fat: 29g | Saturated Fat: 6g | Sodium: 332mg | Potassium: 147mg |

Sugar: 1g | Vitamin A: 570IU | Vitamin C: 0.9mg | Cholesterol: 339mg | Calcium: 53mg | Iron: 1.6mg

32. SCRAMBLED EGGS

Total time: 20 mins

Ingredients:

- 6 tbsp of single- or full-cream milk
- 2 large free range eggs
- a knob of butter

Instructions:

1. 6 tbsp of single cream or full cream milk, 2 big eggs, and a teaspoon of salt should be lightly whisked till the mixture has just one consistency.
2. A small nonstick frying pan should be heated for about a minute before adding a knob of butter and allowing it to melt. The eggs will turn a different color if the butter is allowed to brown.
3. The egg mixture should be added and left to settle for 20 seconds without stirring. Using a wooden spoon, stir while lifpang & folding it over to the pan's bottom.
4. After 10 more seconds, mix it one more and fold it.
5. Continue till the eggs are just just set and still a little runny in spots. Turn on the heat and then step away while you finish cooking.
6. Serve the silky scramble right after after one last stir.

TIPS:

THE BEST RESULTS ARE ATTAINED

Always use a non-stick pan and a wooden spoon, advises chef Bill Granger, for the greatest results and simple cleanup. Avoid over-stirring; imagine these eggs folded rather than scrambled. The eggs should resemble soft curds in texture. The eggs won't cook as well if you cook more than three parts at once since the skillet will be crowded. Cook in two pans rather than one if there will be a larger crowd.

Nutrition: per serving

Kcal 254 Fat 19g Carbs 4g Sugars 0g Saturates 7g Fibre 0g Protein 18g low in salt 0.6g

33. VEGGIE EGG SCRAMBLE

Prep Time: 10 minutes

Cook Time: 10 minutes

Total Time: 20 minutes

Servings: 3 servings

Calories: 178kcal

Ingredients:

- ½ bowl chopped fresh broccoli florets
- ½ bowl diced fresh mushrooms
- ½ bowl diced red pepper
- ½ bowl diced orange pepper
- 1 bowl fresh turnach
- 6 large eggs see note below
- ¼ bowl 1% milk
- ¼ tsp ground black pepper
- ⅛ tsp salt, or as need

- butter flavored cooking spray
- grated cheddar cheese, optional

Instructions:

1. Spray non-stick cooking spray onto a medium skillet that has been heated to medium heat. Broccoli, mushrooms, red pepper, & orange pepper should be added to the skillet. Cook the vegetables for approximately 5 mins, or until they are tender. Turn the turnip over and heat for a further 2 mins to wilt it.
2. In a medium mixing bowl, combine the eggs, milk, pepper, & salt while the vegetables are sautéing. Using a whisk, thoroughly combine the eggs. The eggs get fluffier when cooked as the whisking time increases.
3. Include the vegetables in the egg mixture. Cook for approximately a minute, or until the eggs start to set. Eggs are gently folded over after being pushed into the center of the pan. To enable the liquids to completely cook, tilt the pan gently. Continue till the eggs are almost all set. Add cheese now if you want to. Add to the heat and let stand for a minute. Offer and savor

Notes:

- Egg whites can be substituted for portion of the egg—for 1 egg, use 2 egg whites.
- If cooking for meal preparation, divide into 3 food storage containers & reheat in the microwave for about 30 seconds or in an oven-safe bowl for approximately 5 minutes at 350 degrees.
- Since cheese is optional, it is not included in the nutritional information.

- The dietary advice is based on six eggs.
- Any nutritional information I offer is approximate; real dietary data may change depending on components and portion proportions.
- For a wonderful cutfast, serve with air fryer bagels.

Nutrition:

Serving: 1serving | Calories: 178kcal | Carbohydrates: 6g | Protein: 14g | Fat: 10g | Saturated Fat: 3g | Cholesterol: 372mg | Sodium: 166mg | Potassium: 426mg | Fiber: 1g | Sugar: 4g | Vitamin A: 3165IU | Vitamin C: 80.1mg | Calcium: 98mg | Iron: 2.4mg

34. ALMOND PEANUT BUTTER OATMEAL

Serving: 1

Ingredients:

- ¾ bowl rolled oats(75 g)
- 1 ½ bowls almond milk(360 mL)
- salt, as need
- 2 tbsp peanut butter
- 1 banana, sliced
- cinnamon, as need

Instructions:

1. Bring almond butter to a boil in a small pot. After adding the oats, lower the heat to a simmer. Cook uncovered for about 5 minutes, or until liquid is absorbed. 2. Salt as necessary.

2. Add peanut butter to the oatmeal after placing it in a bowl. Add cinnamon and banana slices as garnish.
3. Enjoy!

Nutrition Info:

Calories 784 Fat 27g Carbs 118g Fiber 17g Sugar 22g Protein 24g

35. CUTFAST KALE MUFFINS

PREP TIME: 10 minutes

COOK TIME: 35 minutes

TOTAL TIME: 45 minutes

INGREDIENTS:

- 1 tbsp olive oil
- 3 cloves garlic, minced
- 1 medium onion, finely chopped
- 8 ounces mushrooms, thinly sliced
- a half-pound of spicy chicken sausage, or sweet if you'd like.
- 3 ounces heat-dried tomatoes, finely chopped
- 2 bowls chopped kale
- 8 ounces feta cheese, crumbled
- Pam cooking spray
- 12- bowl muffin pan
- 1 ½ bowls egg substitute, or 6 eggs

INSTRUCTIONS:

1. turn the oven on to 350 degrees.

2. After adding the oil, sauté the onion for 4 mins. Stir in the garlic and cook for a further minute.
3. Cook for 5 mins after adding the mushrooms. Once added, simmer the chicken sausage for 6 mins, or until fully cooked. Slice the sausage into little pieces. Add the heat-dried tomatoes and completely combine.
4. Kale should cook for around 2 mins or until it begins to slightly wilt.
5. Stir in feta after removing from heat
6. Spray muffin tin, then equally distribute contents into each basin.
7. Fill each bowl with an equal quantity of egg, stopping just shy of the rim.
8. Bake for 25 to 30 mins, or until the eggs are set.

NOTES:

Can be stored in a container that is airtight for up to 3-4 days in the refrigerator.

can also be frozen. Before freezing, separately cover each egg dish with aluminum foil and plastic wrap. Reheat for 30 to 45 seconds in a microwave or toaster oven.

NUTRITION INFORMATION:

Calories 146 Total Fat 8g Saturated Fat 3g Unsaturated Fat 0g Cholesterol 30mg Sodium 489mg Carbohydrates 8g Fiber 1g Sugar 5g Protein 10g

36. CHOCOLATE OVERNIGHT OATS

Prep Time: 5 min

Cook Time: 0 min

Refrigerate: 4 Hours

Total Time: 4 hours 5 minutes

Servings: 6

Calories: 257 kcal

Ingredients:

- 2 bowl old-fashioned rolled oats
- 3 tbsp of unsweetened cocoa powder or raw cacao powder
- 1 tbsp chia seeds
- 2 bowl non-dairy milk
- 2/3 bowl yogurt coconut or greek
- 2 tsp pure vanilla remove
- 1/3 bowl pure maple syrup
- 1/4 cup chopped dark sugar-free chocolate or dark micro chocolate chips

Instructions:

1. To a bowl for mixing, add all the ingredients. After fully mixing, divide the mixture into dishes or containers.
2. Place for at least 4 hours or overnight in the refrigerator.
3. For a quick breakfast, serve chilled. Enjoy!

4. keeps good for a maximum of five days in the refrigerator.

Notes:

- Be careful to refrigerate the oats for at least 4 hours, if not overnight. To become really soft, these oats require more time to absorb milk.
- You may substitute honey or Lakanto Monk Fruit Sweetener for maple syrup if you don't have any on hand. Agave is a suitable substitute for honey for vegans.
- For this recipe, rolled oats work best because of their tendency to be a little softer. For this dish, we have not tested using instant oats. However, the texture will be different if you use quick oats.
- Make sure the oats are not cross-contaminated with gluten if you follow a gluten-free diet. Use oats devoid of gluten.
- Use non-dairy milk, non-dairy yogurt, & dairy-free chocolate chips for a vegan version.
- Fruits like a banana, strawberry, or blueberry are possible additions.

Nutrition:

Calories: 257kcal | Carbohydrates: 41g | Protein: 8g | Fat: 7g | Saturated Fat: 3g | Trans Fat: 1g | Cholesterol: 4mg | Sodium: 56mg | Potassium: 339mg | Fiber: 5g | Sugar: 14g | Vitamin A: 337IU | Vitamin C: 6mg | Calcium: 193mg | Iron: 2mg

37. PUMPKIN MUFFINS

Prep Time: 20 minutes

Cook Time: 22 minutes

Total Time: 42 minutes

Yield: 12

INGREDIENTS:

- 1 3/4 bowls all purpose flour
- 1 bowl sugar
- 1/2 bowl dark brown sugar
- 1 tsp baking soda
- 1/2 tsp salt
- 2 tsp cinnamon
- 1/4 tsp ground cloves
- 1/4 tsp nutmeg
- 2 eggs
- 1 15 ounce can pure pumpkin puree
- 1/2 bowl coconut oil, melted
- 1 tsp vanilla remove.

INSTRUCTIONS:

1. Put 12 paper liners into each well of a standard-sized muffin baking pan and preheat the oven to 375 degrees.
2. In a medium bowl, combine the spices, salt, baking soda, and flour after measuring each ingredient out. Place aside.
3. Combine the eggs, pumpkin puree, coconut oil, and vanilla extract in a separate dish.

4. Stir together the dry ingredients after adding the heated ingredients. Just whisk everything into the batter until it is well combined without over-mixing.
5. To properly pour the batter into each well, a sizable scoop (like an ice cream scoop) might be useful. They'll be almost full. Your muffins will have a wonderful fluffy dome as a result of this.
6. After 20 to 22 mins of baking, a toothpick inserted into the centre of a muffin should come out clean.

NUTRITION:

SERVING SIZE: 1 MuffinCALORIES: 267SUGAR: 25gSODIUM: 209mgFAT: 10gSATURATED FAT: 7.8gUNSATURATED FAT: 1.3gTRANS FAT: 0gCARBOHYDRATES: 41gFIBER: 1.8gPROTEIN: 3.4gCHOLESTEROL: 31mg

38. ALMOND OATMEALS

Prep Time: 5 minutes

Cook Time: 10 minutes

Total Time: 15 minutes

Servings: 4

Calories: 299kcal

Ingredients:

- 2 bowl water
- 1 tsp cinnamon
- 1 bowl oats, dry
- 1/2 bowl almonds, sliced
- 2 tbsp honey

- Serve With
- 2 medium apple

Instructions:

1. In a saucepan, mix the water and cinnamon. Turn up the heat. Add the oats and stir once it starts to boil.
2. Low-heat setting. Cook while periodically stirring until the desired consistency is reached.
3. Add honey and almonds on the top. Apple slices should be served on the side.

Nutrition:

Calories: 299kcal | Carbohydrates: 50g | Protein: 9g | Fat: 9g | Saturated Fat: 1g | Sodium: 7mg | Fiber: 8g | Sugar: 19g

39. MUSHROOM FRITTATA

Prep Time: 20 mins

Cook Time: 20 mins

Rest time: 10 mins

Total Time: 50 mins

Servings: 8 slices

Calories: 154kcal

INGREDIENTS:

- 2 tbsp olive oil
- 16 oz button mushrooms sliced
- 8 large eggs
- ¼ bowl sour cream

- ¼ tsp sea salt
- ¼ tsp black pepper
- ¼ tsp dried thyme
- ½ bowl chopped scallions green parts
- ½ bowl dry-grated Parmesan cheese
- Olive oil spray

INSTRUCTIONS:

1. Set the oven to 400 degrees Fahrenheit. Heat a pie bowl of 9 inches in diameter in the oven.
2. Over medium heat, warm the olive oil in a large skillet. the mushrooms are added. Cook the mushrooms for approximately 10 minutes, stirring periodically, or until they are tender and browned and any moisture has disappeared.
3. Salt, pepper, thyme, and sour cream should all be mixed into the eggs. With a spatula, incorporate the cheese and scallions.
4. Utilizing oven mitts, transfer the heated pie bowl to the oven. Spray it with olive oil and set it on a heatproof surface (or brush it with olive oil). To the baking bowl, add the mushrooms. On top, pour the egg mixture. light blending
5. Re-enter the oven with the baking basin. A knife placed in the middle of the frittata should come out clean after 20 to 25 minutes of baking, when the frittata's edges are golden brown and puffy.
6. The frittata should cool for 10 mins before cutting it into 8 pieces and serving.

NOTES:

Make careful to oil the bottom, sides, and top of the pie plate completely because the mixture will rise very high when you add the ingredients. You might also place the pie plate on a large cookie sheet to collect any drips.

NUTRITION PER SERVING:

Serving: 1slice | Calories: 154kcal | Carbohydrates: 3g | Protein: 10g | Saturated Fat: 4g | Sodium: 240mg | Fat: 11g | Fiber: 1g | Sugar: 2g

LUNCH

40. CUCUMBER TUNA SALAD

Prep: 10 minutes

Total: 10 minutes

Servings: 4 people

Ingredients:

- 1 ½ bowls cucumber chopped
- ½ bowl red onions chopped
- 1 bowl red bell pepper chopped
- 2 medium avocado peeled, pitted and chopped
- 2 cans 12oz flaked light tuna, drained
- 1 tbsp chives chopped
- 1 tbsp lemon juice
- 2 tbsp olive oil
- Salt and freshly ground black pepper

Instructions:

1. Cucumber, red onions, bell pepper, avocado, drained tuna, and chives should all be combined in a large salad dish.
2. Pour the freshly squeezed lemon juice, olive oil, salt, and black pepper into a mason jar. Everything should be combined by whisking.
3. Pour over the salad after tasting to determine the seasoning.
4. Throw in a mix and relish!

Nutrition Information:

Serving: 1/6 Calories: 205kcal (10%) Carbohydrates: 9g (3%) Protein: 20g (40%) Fat: 11g (17%) Saturated Fat: 2g (13%) Cholesterol: 32mg (11%) Sodium: 427mg (19%) Fiber: 5g (21%) Sugar: 3g (3%)

41. PARMESAN ROASTED CAULIFLOWER

Servings: 6

Ingredients:

- 7 bowls cauliflower florets(2 kg)
- 1 tbsp olive oil
- 1 bowl italian breadcrumb(115 g)
- ½ tsp garlic powder
- ½ tsp salt
- ½ bowl grated parmesan cheese(55 g)

Preparation:

1. Set the oven to 425 °F (220 °F).

2. Olive oil and cauliflower florets should be combined thoroughly in a dish or zip-top bag.
3. Add the salt, Parmesan, breadcrumbs, and garlic powder. Stir to ensure complete coating.
4. Spread the cauliflower on a baking sheet that has been greased and coated with foil.
5. For 20 mins, bake. Bake the cauliflower for 10 more minutes after stirring.
6. Enjoy!

Nutrition Info:

Calories 230 Fat 6g Carbs 34g Fiber 5g Sugar 6g Protein 11g

42. CAULIFLOWER MUSHROOM SOUP

Prep Time: 10 minutes

Cook Time: 50 minutes

Total Time: 1 hour

Yield: 4 servings

INGREDIENTS:

For the soup

- 2 pounds of one medium-sized head of cauliflower, divided into big florets.
- 2 large shallots, peeled & cut into quarters
- 1 tbsp fresh thyme leaves, stripped to woody stem, or 1/2 tsp dried thyme
- A pound and a half of cleaned and cut-in-half crimini mushrooms
- 4 garlic cloves, peeled & tough ends trimmed

- 1/2 tsp fresh cracked black pepper
- 1 tsp sea salt
- Sufficient to thoroughly cover vegetables for roasting with 3–4 tbsp of olive oil or avocado oil
- 1/2 bowl raw cashews
- 5 1/2 bowls broth
- 1 tbsp coconut aminos or tamari
- 1 tbsp nutritional yeast
- 1 tbsp aged balsamic vinegar or balsamic reduction
- salt as need – I used about 1 1/2 tsp

For the garnish

- reserved roasted veggies
- aged balsamic or balsamic reduction
- fresh thyme
- black pepper

INSTRUCTIONS:

1. Set oven to 400 degrees Fahrenheit.
2. To a large sheet pan, add cleaned garlic cloves, quartered shallots, halves of mushrooms, and shallots. Sprinkle generously with salt, pepper, & around 3 to 4 tablespoons of olive oil.
3. After transferring, roast the vegetables in the oven for approximately 30 minutes, stirring regularly, or until they are tender and beginning to starch. Roast for a another 10-15 minutes, raising the heat to 475, or until everything is fully caramelized.
4. Place in the oven, saving a few tiny, crispy cauliflower and mushroom pieces for the soup's optional garnish. In order to make cleanup easier and collect all the umami-rich flavor pieces for the soup, add 1 1/2 cups

of broth to the sheet pan and scrape off any browned bits that have remained there. In a sizable soup pot, combine the entire contents of the roasting tray with the rest of the broth, raw cashews, nutritional yeast, coconut aminos or tamari, & balsamic vinegar. Immediately after bringing to a boil, rapidly lower heat to a simmer.

5. The cauliflower should be completely tender and the cashews puffed up after about 10 minutes of simmering with the lid on.

6. In a blender, puree the soup (if necessary, in stages) until it is silky smooth. Return to the pot and add salt and pepper as desired. Serve with fresh thyme, crushed black pepper, and any reserved roasted vegetables.

NOTES:

To make this recipe nut-free, simply omit the cashews or swap your chosen non-dairy milk or creamer for 1 1/2 cups of the broth.

Nutrition Info:

Total Fat 19g Cholesterol 0mg Sodium 1646.8mg Total Carbohydrate 26.2g Dietary Fiber 4.9g Sugars 9.9g Protein 9.8g Vitamin A 1.5µg Vitamin C 73.6mg Calcium 75.6mg Iron 2.6mg Vitamin D 0.2µg Magnesium 83.4mg

43. CREAMY CAULIFLOWER SOUP

Prep Time: 15 minutes

Cook Time: 55 minutes

Total Time: 1 hour 10 minutes

Yield: 4 bowls

INGREDIENTS:

- 1 large head cauliflower (about 2 pounds), cut into bite-size florets
- 3 tbsp extra-virgin olive oil, divided
- Fine sea salt
- 1 medium red onion, chopped
- 2 cloves garlic, pressed or minced
- 4 bowls (32 ounces) vegetable broth
- 2 tbsp unsalted butter
- 1 tbsp fresh lemon juice, or more if needed
- Scant ¼ tsp ground nutmeg
- For garnish: 2 tbsp finely chopped fresh flat-leaf parsley, chives and/or green onions

INSTRUCTIONS:

1. Set the oven's temperature to 425 degrees. For simpler cleanup, you may line a large baking sheet with a rim with parchment paper.
2. Toss the cauliflower on the baking pan with 2 tbsp of the olive oil so it is thinly and evenly covered. Sprinkle a little salt over the cauliflower after placing it in a single layer. Bake for 25 to 35 mins, stirring halfway

through, until the edges of the cauliflower are tender and caramelized.

3. When the cauliflower is almost done, heat the remaining 1 tbsp of olive oil over medium heat in a Dutch oven or soup pot until shimmering. Add 14 teaspoon salt and the onion. Cook for 5 to 7 minutes, stirring periodically, till the onion is cooked and beginning to become translucent.

4. After adding the garlic, simmer it for about 30 seconds while stirring continually before adding the stock.

5. For garnish, save 4 of the most attractive roasted cauliflower florets. Add the leftover cauliflower to the pot after that. The mixture should be heated to a simmer over medium-high heat, then the heat should be adjusted as needed to maintain a moderate simmer. To allow the flavors to mingle, cook for 20 minutes while stirring periodically.

6. Take the soup pot from the heat when the soup has finished cooking and allow it to cool for a few mins. The heated soup should then be gently transferred, maybe in portions, to a blender. (Avoid filling the soup up past the maximum fill line or it could overflow.)

7. Blend in the butter until well-combined. Blend again after including the nutmeg and lemon juice. If more salt is needed, add it (I often add another 1/4 to 3/4 tsp, depending on the broth). Once the soup has been adequately seasoned, it tastes fantastic! If you think it needs more zing, you may also add a bit extra lemon juice. Blend once more.

8. One roasted cauliflower floret and a garnish of chopped parsley, green onion, and/or chives should be placed on top of each individual soup dish. For roughly four days under refrigeration or for several

months in the freezer, this soup stores nicely when covered.

NOTES:

MAKE IT VEGAN OR DAIRY FREE: Butter can be replaced with cashews. Cashews should be soaked for four hours, then drained and rinsed (You may omit this step if you have a powerful blender, such as a Vitamix or Blendtec.). When you would add the butter, add the cashews instead.

Nutrition Facts:

Total Fat 17g Saturated Fat 5.4g Trans Fat 0g Polyunsaturated Fat 1.4g Monounsaturated Fat 9.3g

44. CAULIFLOWER MASH

PREP: 15 MINS

COOK: 20 MINS

TOTAL: 35 MINS

SERVES: 8

INGREDIENTS:

- 1 large head of cauliflower divided into florets, weighing approximately 3 pounds (1 1/2 kg)
- 3 tbsp unsalted butter
- 3 tbsp sour cream
- 6 cloves garlic divided
- 1/4 bowl parmesan cheese
- Salt and black pepper as need

INSTRUCTIONS:

1. Over a large saucepan of boiling water, place the cauliflower in a steamer. Until soft, steam for 15 mins. Alternately, cook cauliflower in salted water for ten minutes, or until tender when pierced with a fork. Drain and take. Put aside and cover with a lid.
2. Heat the butter in the same pan at a medium-high temperature. Garlic is cooked till aromatic (about 1 minute).
3. On high speed, puree the cauliflower & garlic in the food processor until smooth. The size of your processor may need you to perform this in groups of two or three.
4. Add the garlic and the pureed cauliflower to the saucepan. Add the Parmesan cheese, sour cream, and salt & pepper to taste.

NOTES:

Cauliflower rice will save you time in the kitchen! The rice should be fork-soft after being steamed or sautéed in a skillet with some water.

NUTRITION:

Calories: 59kcal | Carbohydrates: 2g | Protein: 1g | Fat: 5g | Saturated Fat: 3g | Cholesterol: 13mg | Sodium: 61mg | Potassium: 54mg | Vitamin A: 165IU | Vitamin C: 7.2mg | Calcium: 51mg | Iron: 0.1mg

45. CURRIED EGG SALAD

PREP TIME: 10 minutes

COOK TIME: 20 minutes

TOTAL TIME: 30 minutes

INGREDIENTS:

- 6 large eggs
- 1 stalk celery, finely diced (about 1/4 bowl)
- 1/4 bowl reduced-fat mayonnaise
- 1 tbsp Dijon mustard
- 1 1/4 tsp curry powder
- 1/4 tsp kosher salt
- 1/4 tsp black pepper

INSTRUCTIONS:

1. A big pot should have eggs in the bottom, and the water should be chilly.
2. On a high heat setting, bring water to a boil. The eggs should rest in the pan for 20 minutes after the heat has been turned off.
3. Prepare the remaining ingredients while you wait and put them in a medium bowl.
4. Drain the eggs & give them a cold water rinse after 20 minutes.
5. Chop the peeled eggs into small pieces.
6. Toss the dish thoroughly after adding the diced eggs.
7. Add more salt & black pepper as desired to season. If you want it a bit creamier, you can also add another tablespoon of mayonnaise.

NOTES:

- I make mine using reduced-fat mayonnaise, but you could also use regular mayo, plain Greek yogurt, or a mixture of the two.
- For a little bit of crunch, I include celery to this recipe, but you may omit it for a smoother one.
- If you'd like, you may also include some finely chopped pimientos or red pepper. If you have some on hand, I adore adding or topping it with a few snips of fresh chives.
- I like to serve it with a little more freshly cracked black pepper, red onion slices, and spicy sauce. Sriracha sauce would be fantastic as well!
- This dish can be served open-faced on toast (as seen in the photo), as a lettuce wrap, as an egg salad sandwich, or simply with crackers and vegetables. Like I do with my typical egg salad, it would also be wonderful as an egg salad BLT sandwich.
- In the refrigerator, this egg salad lasts for two to three days when covered.

NUTRITION INFORMATION:

Amount Per Serving: CALORIES: 161TOTAL FAT: 12gSATURATED FAT: 3gCHOLESTEROL: 279mgSODIUM: 259mgFIBER: 1gSUGAR: 1gPROTEIN: 10g

46. DIJON POTATO SALAD

Prep: 10 mins

Total: 30 mins

Servings: 4

Ingredients:

- 1 1/2 pounds red fresh potatoes, scrubbed and halved (quartered if large)
- 1 tbsp white-wine vinegar
- 1 tbsp Dijon mustard
- Coarse salt and ground pepper
- 2 tbsp olive oil
- 1/2 bowl chopped fresh parsley

Instructions:

1. Place a steamer basket in a saucepan that is 1 inch deep with water. Gently bring to a boil. include potatoes With the lid on, simmer for 15 to 20 minutes, stirring regularly, just until soft.
2. Combine vinegar and Dijon in a serving dish; season with salt & pepper. Toss in the hot, cooked potatoes. Allow to cool, periodically tossing.
3. Cooled potato mixture is combined with oil and parsley. Add salt and pepper, then toss.

47. CARROT SWEET POTATO SOUP

Servings: 8

Total Time: 45 Minutes

INGREDIENTS:

- 4 tbsp unsalted butter
- 2 medium yellow onions, chopped
- 1 tbsp curry powder, + a bit more for serving
- 1 pound carrots, peeled and chopped into 1 inch pieces
- 1½ pounds sweet potatoes (about 2 small), peeled and chopped into 1-inch pieces
- 8 bowls chicken broth, best quality such as Swanson
- 1¾ tsp salt
- 1 tart yet sweet apple (such as Honeycrisp or Fuji), peeled and chopped
- 2 tbsp honey
- Freshly ground black pepper

INSTRUCTIONS:

1. Melt the butter in a big pan over moderate heat. Add the onions & sauté them for approximately 10 minutes, stirring regularly, until they are tender and transparent. Avoid browning. Cook for another minute after adding the curry powder.
2. Bring to a boil after adding the salt, chicken stock, and carrots and sweet potatoes. Vegetables should be covered and simmered for around 25 minutes on low heat. Add honey and apples after stirring. Using a stick blender, puree the soup till it is smooth & creamy. (Alternatively, briefly chill the soup before pulsing it

in batches in a blender. To enable the steam to escape, be sure to leave the lid's hole unplugged & cover with a kitchen towel.) Add salt, pepper, and more honey as desired to taste. Pour the soup into bowls and, if desired, top with additional curry powder. (Note: You may need to add extra water to thin down the soup if it thickens as it sits.)

3. Freezer-Friendly Advice: You may freeze the soup for up to three months. The soup should be defrosted in the fridge for 12 hours before being heated through on the stovetop.

NUTRITION INFORMATION:

Calories: 277 Fat: 9g Saturated fat: 4g Carbohydrates: 42g Sugar: 18g Fiber: 5g Protein: 8g Sodium: 941mg Cholesterol: 22mg

48. CREAMY SALMON SALAD

PREP TIME: 15 mins

COOK TIME: 20 mins

CHILL TIME: 10 mins

TOTAL TIME: 45 mins

SERVINGS: 4 servings

INGREDIENTS:

FOR THE SALMON

- 1 ¼ pounds salmon filet
- ½ tbsp olive oil
- 1 tsp smoked paprika

- as needed, freshly ground black pepper & kosher salt

FOR THE DRESSING

- ⅓ bowl mayonnaise
- ½ lemon, zested and juiced (about ½ tbsp of zest and 1 ½ tbsp juice)
- 2 tsp Dijon mustard
- 1 garlic clove, minced
- kosher salt & freshly ground black pepper, as need

FOR THE SALAD

- ½ small red onion, finely diced
- 3 large rabowles, grated
- 2 stalks celery, small diced
- 2 tbsp finely chopped fresh dill
- 2 tbsp finely chopped fresh chives

INSTRUCTIONS :

1. Salmon preparation. Set the oven's temperature to 375°F (190°C). Salmon should be placed on a parchment-lined baking pan. Olive oil, smoked paprika, salt, & pepper are used to season the fish.
2. Salmon is baked and flaked. Depending on size and thickness, bake the salmon for 16 to 15 mins, or till it flakes easily with a fork. Before cutting up and arranging the salmon in a plate, allow it to reach room temperature. The flakes salmon should be refrigerated for five to ten minutes.
3. Slice or dice the produce. Add the onion, rabbowl, celery, dill, & chives to the flakes salmon as garnish.

4. Construct the dressing. Make the dressing in a separate, little bowl. Mayonnaise, lemon juice, mustard, garlic, salt, & pepper are all combined.
5. Mix everything together. Sprinkle the salad with the dressing, then give it a quick swirl to combine.
6. Serve the chilled salmon salad directly from the dish, on leaves of butter lettuce, or as a sandwich or wrap.

NUTRITION:

CALORIES: 361kcal, CARBOHYDRATES: 4g, PROTEIN: 29g, FAT: 25g, SATURATED FAT: 4g, POLYUNSATURATED FAT: 12g, MONOUNSATURATED FAT: 7g, TRANS FAT: 0.04g, CHOLESTEROL: 86mg, SODIUM: 227mg, POTASSIUM: 820mg, FIBER: 1g, SUGAR: 1g, VITAMIN A: 491iu, VITAMIN C: 11mg, CALCIUM: 40mg, IRON: 2mg

49. BAKED DIJON SALMON

PREP TIME: 5 mins

COOK TIME: 20 mins

TOTAL TIME: 25 mins

SERVINGS: 5 serving

INGREDIENTS:

- 1 1/2 lbs salmon, King, Sockeye or Coho salmon
- 1/4 bowl fresh parsley, finely chopped
- 1/4 bowl Dijon mustard
- 1 tbsp lemon juice
- 1 tbsp avocado oil
- 3 garlic cloves, finely chopped
- salt and pepper

INSTRUCTIONS:

1. Set your oven's temperature to 375 degrees Fahrenheit. In a small bowl, combine the mustard, parsley, oil, garlic, and lemon juice.
2. Spread the herbed mustard mixture generously over the salmon before placing it on a parchment-lined baking sheet.
3. Depending on size & thickness, bake the salmon for 18 to 20 mins before slicing it into individual servings and serving right away.

TIPS:

Instead of using one large salmon fillet, you could simply use 4-6 smaller pieces.

NUTRITION:

CALORIES: 249.7kcal, CARBOHYDRATES: 1.9g, PROTEIN: 30.5g, FAT: 13.4g, SATURATED FAT: 1.7g, CHOLESTEROL: 87.1mg, SODIUM: 371mg, FIBER: 0.5g, SUGAR: 0.3g

50. DIJON CHICKEN THIGHS

Prep Time: 5 mins

Cook Time: 25 mins

Total Time: 30 mins

Servings; 4 servings

EQUIPMENT:

3 quart baking bowl

INGREDIENTS:

- 1 ½ – ¾ pounds (680 g) boneless, skinless chicken thighs (6-8 pieces)
- ¾ bowl (60 g) sliced shallots (about 2 large)

Dijon marinade

- 2 tbsp (30 g) Dijon mustard
- 2 tbsp (30 g) tomato paste
- 1 lemon, juiced, approximately ¼ bowl

- 2 tbsp (30 ml) extra virgin olive oil
- Freshly chopped thyme, 1 tsp (15 g), or dried thyme, 1 tsp
- 1-2 garlic cloves, finely chopped or grated
- 1 tsp kosher salt
- ½ tsp freshly ground black pepper, or as need
- ½ tsp crushed red chili pepper

INSTRUCTIONS:

1. Set the oven's temperature to 425.
2. In a medium baking dish with a capacity of about 3 quarts, place the chicken. For simpler cleanup, if your pan or bowl is not nonstick, spray it with cooking spray or line it with a piece of aluminum foil.
3. Blend the marinade.
4. In a medium bowl, mix the tomato paste, mustard, lemon juice, olive oil, thyme, garlic, salt, pepper, & chili.
5. Put the chicken together and bake it.
6. The chicken should be covered once the marinade has been poured over it. Place the shallots all over the chicken, sprinkling them occasionally in the spaces between the thighs. While the covered shallots bake and soften, some of the ununcovered shallots will crisp and brown.
7. Before baking, the chicken & marinade can be covered and kept in the fridge for a maximum of 24 hours.
8. Bake the chicken for 25 to 30 mins, or until the juices are bubbling and the chicken is opaque. Serve hot.

NOTES:

- Plan ahead: When it's time to make supper, simply throw the chicken in the oven after marinating it in the mustard mixture over the night.
- Place the raw chicken in a freezer-safe bag and freeze. Bake after thawing in the fridge for the night.
- Another fresh fragrant herb, such as rosemary or oregano, can be used in place of fresh thyme. If using dried herbs, cut the quantity in half.

NUTRITION:

Calories: 313kcal | Carbohydrates: 11g | Protein: 35g | Fat: 14g | Saturated Fat: 3g | Sodium: 891mg | Potassium: 682mg | Fiber: 2g | Sugar: 5g | Vitamin A: 330IU | Vitamin C: 8mg | Calcium: 51mg | Iron: 3mg

51. HERB PORK CHOPS

Prep Time: 10 mins

Cook Time: 25 mins

Total Time: 35 mins

Servings: 4

Yield: 4 servings

Ingredients:

- 4 thick-cut pork chops
- 1 tsp Montreal steak seasoning, or as need
- ½ bowl butter, divided
- 2 ½ tbsp all-purpose flour, or as needed
- 1 tbsp dried basil

- 1 tsp instant beef bouillon granules
- 1 tsp freshly ground black pepper
- 2 bowls milk

Instructions:

1. Montreal steak seasoning should be spread on all sides of the pork chops.
2. 2 tbsp of butter should be melted in a big pan over medium heat. Chops should be cooked in heated butter for 7 -10 minutes on each side, or until browned and just pink in the middle. In the middle, an instant-read thermometer should register at least 145 degrees Fahrenheit (63 degrees C). As required, add additional butter to the pan so that, after the chops are done cooking, there are about 3 tbsp of pan drippings left. Once the pork chops have been removed to a platter, re-heat the skillet over medium-high.
3. In a bowl, combine the flour, basil, & beef bouillon. Cook for one minute after adding black pepper to the skillet with the pan drippings. Add the flour mixture and whisk continuously while cooking for 2 minutes or until browned. Add milk to the flour mixture and whisk continuously for 4 to 6 mins, or until the dough thickens and bubbles. Serve the pork chops with sauce.

Nutrition Facts:

601 Calories 44gFat 11gCarbs 40gProtein

52. TACO CHICKEN

Yield: 6 SERVINGS

Prep time: 15 MINUTES

Cook time: 15 MINUTES

Total time: 30 MINUTES

INGREDIENTS:

- 2 tsp chili powder
- 1 tsp ground cumin
- 1 tsp smoked paprika
- 1 tsp dried oregano
- 1/2 tsp garlic powder
- as needed, freshly ground black pepper & kosher salt
- 1 and a half pounds of skinless, boneless chicken thighs
- 1 tbsp canola oil
- 12 mini flour tortillas, warmed
- 1 bowl pico de gallo, homemade or store-bought
- 1 avocado, halved, peeled, seeded and diced
- 1/2 bowl chopped fresh cilantro leaves
- 1 lime, cut into wedges

INSTRUCTIONS:

1. Mix chili powder, cumin, paprika, oregano, garlic powder, 1 tsp salt, and 1/2 teaspoon pepper in a small bowl. Chicken is seasoned with a variety of chili powders.
2. Large cast iron skillet with canola oil heated to medium-high heat. Add the chicken to the skillet in a

thin layer while cooking in batches & cook for 4-5 minutes each side, or until golden brown and well cooked, with an internal temperature of 165 degrees F. Slice into bite-sized pieces after allowing to cool.

3. Chicken should be served in tortillas with pico de gallo, avocado, cilantro, and lime on top.

53. BROILED FISH FILLET

Prep/Total Time: 20 min.

Makes: 4 servings

Ingredients:

- 4 fillets of red snapper, trout, catfish, or orange roughy (6 ounces every)
- 6 tbsp butter, melted, divided
- 1 tbsp all-purpose flour
- Paprika
- Juice of 1 lemon
- 1 tbsp minced fresh parsley
- 2 tsp Worcestershire sauce

Instructions:

1. Place the fish on a broiler rack that has been spray-coated. 3 tbsp of butter should be drizzled over the fillets before they are floured and paprika-dusted.
2. 5-6 inches from the fire for 5 minutes, or until the fish just starts to turn brown. Pour over fish the mixture of lemon juice, parsley, Worcestershire sauce, and remaining butter. 5 more minutes of broiling is required or until the salmon flakes readily.

Nutrition Facts:

1 fillet: 292 calories, 147mg cholesterol, 3g carbohydrate (1g sugars, 0 fiber), 272mg sodium, 28g protein, 18g fat (11g saturated fat).

54. YUMMY CHICKEN BITE

Servings: 2

Ingredients:

- 2 chicken breasts
- 1 egg, beaten
- 2 bowls panko breadcrumbs(100 g)
- salt
- pepper
- 4 tbsp soy sauce
- 4 tbsp honey
- 4 cloves garlic, crushed
- 2 tbsp hoisin sauce
- 1 tbsp sriracha
- 1 tbsp grated ginger
- spring onion, for garnish
- sesame seed, for garnish

Preparation:

1. Oven should be heated to 400°F (200°C).
2. Chicken breasts should be cut into bite-sized pieces.
3. Chicken pieces are dipped in egg mixture and then panko-coated.
4. Sprinkle salt and pepper over the breaded chicken before placing it on a baking pan.
5. Bake for 20 mins, or until well cooked and golden.

6. In a saucepan, mix the soy sauce, honey, garlic, hoisin sauce, sriracha, & grated ginger. Bring to a boil and then heat.
7. Chicken bits should be completely covered with sauce before serving.
8. Serve right away with sesame seeds and finely sliced spring onion.
9. Enjoy!

Nutrition:

Calories 850 Fat 12g Carbs 121g Fiber 4g Sugar 52g Protein 62g

55. GRILLED CHICKEN BREASTS

CAL/SERV: 190

YIELDS: 4 SERVINGS

PREP TIME: 0 HOURS 15 MINS

TOTAL TIME: 0 HOURS 45 MINS

INGREDIENTS:

- 1/4 c. balsamic vinegar
- 3 tbsp. extra-virgin olive oil
- 2 tbsp. brown sugar
- 3 cloves garlic, minced
- 1 tsp. dried thyme
- 1 tsp. dried rosemary
- 4 chicken breasts
- Kosher salt
- Freshly ground black pepper
- Freshly chopped parsley, for garnish

INSTRUCTIONS:

1. Mix the balsamic vinegar, olive oil, brown sugar, garlic, & dried herbs in a medium bowl. Add enough of salt and pepper to taste. 14 of the bowl should be set aside.
2. Chicken should be added to the bowl, then mixed. Allow to marinate for up to a day, but no more than 20 mins.
3. Set the grill to medium-high heat. Add the chicken, and cook it on the grill for 6 minutes per side, basting it with the marinade you saved.
4. Before serving, garnish with parsley.

Nutrition (per serving):

190 calories, 4 grammes of carbs, 3 grammes of sugar, 1 gramme of saturated fat, 307 milligrammes of sodium, 27 grammes of protein, and 2 grammes of fibre.

56. CHILLI LEMON TILAPIA

PREP TIME: 10 mins

COOK TIME: 10 mins

SERVINGS: 4 servings

CALORIES: 399

INGREDIENTS:

- 6 tilapia fillets about 1.5 ounce every
- ¼ bowl melted butter
- 8 cloves garlic minced
- 2 tsp smoked paprika

- 1 ½ tsp chili powder
- 1 ¼ tsp cumin powder
- 1 tsp ground pepper
- Salt as need
- 1 tsp lemon zest
- 1 tbsp lemon juice
- 4-5 lemon slices
- 2 tbsp chicken stock (optional)

For Garnish

- Chopped Cilantro

INSTRUCTIONS:

1. If you've ever wondered how to bake tilapia, it just requires three easy steps.
2. Melted butter is blended with garlic, smoked paprika, chili powder, cumin powder, ground pepper, salt, and lemon juice (not seen in movie).
3. Pour it over the tilapia fish that is arranged in a row on the baking sheet (greased with butter or oil).
4. The fish should bake for around 10 minutes at 400F. Your fish's size will affect how long it takes to cook.
5. When finished, top the baked tilapia with cilantro that has been finely chopped and serve it right away over rice, quinoa, or couscous.
6. Ideally, serve hot.

NOTES:

- Add 2 tbsp of chicken stock to one corner of the baking sheet halfway through cooking time to avoid the spices from burning in the oven. You will observe how moist and chicken tilapia turns out of the oven even if this step is optional. Before placing the fish in the oven, you can add chicken stock, but doing so may dilute the spice rub mixture, causing the fish to lose part of its flavor into the liquid.

NUTRITION:

Calories: 399kcal Carbohydrates: 14g Protein: 53g Fat: 16g Saturated Fat: 8g Cholesterol: 158mg Sodium: 262mg Potassium: 991mg Fiber: 3g Sugar: 3g Vitamin A: 1095IU Vitamin C: 61.2mg Calcium: 74mg Iron: 3mg

57. GARLIC SHRIMP

Prep Time: 15 mins

Cook Time: 10 mins

Total Time: 25 mins

Servings: 4

Ingredients:

- 1 ½ tbsp olive oil
- 1 pound shrimp, peeled and deveined
- salt as need
- 6 cloves garlic, finely minced
- ¼ tsp red pepper flakes
- 3 tbsp lemon juice
- 1 tbsp caper brine
- 2 tbsp cold butter, cut into 4 equal pieces, divided
- ⅓ bowl chopped flat-leaf parsley, divided
- 1 tsp water, or as needed

Instructions:

1. The olive oil should be heated over high heat in a big, heavy pan until it just begins to smoke. On the bottom of the pan, spread out the shrimp evenly, and cook for 1 minute without stirring.
2. Salt the shrimp, then heat and toss them for about a minute, or until they start to turn pink.
3. Cook and stir for one minute after adding the garlic & red pepper flakes.
4. Add 1 tablespoon of butter, the lemon juice, the caper brine, and half of the parsley. About 1 minute will pass after the butter has melted.
5. Add the remaining three slices of butter while lowering the heat to low. Cook and stir for 2 to 3 mins, or until sauce is thick, butter has melted, and shrimp are pink and opaque.
6. Remove the shrimp using a large spoon, then put them in a bowl. Continue to simmer the butter sauce for another 2 minutes, adding water 1 tsp at a time if it becomes too thick. Use salt to season.
7. Serve the shrimp with the pan sauce and the final bit of parsley on top.

Nutrition Facts (per serving):

196Calories 12gFat 3gCarbs 19gProtein

58. CHOCOLATE AVOCADO PUDDING

Prep Time: 10 mins

Additional Time: 30 mins

Total Time: 40 mins

Servings: 4

Ingredients:

- 2 large avocados - peeled, pitted, and cubed
- ½ bowl unsweetened cocoa powder
- ½ bowl brown sugar
- ⅓ bowl coconut milk
- 2 tsp vanilla remove
- 1 pinch ground cinnamon

Instructions:

1. Avocados, cocoa powder, brown sugar, coconut milk, vanilla, & cinnamon are all blended together until they are completely smooth. Transfer the pudding to a lidded container, then chill in the fridge for about 30 mins.

Nutrition Facts (per serving):

400Calories 26gFat 46gCarbs 5gProtein

59. FROZEN BERRY YOGURT

Prep:2 mins

Serves: 4

Ingredients:

- 250g frozen mixed berry
- 250g 0%-fat Greek yogurt
- 1 tbsp honey or agave syrup

Instructions:

1. In a food processor, mix the berries, yogurt, honey, or agave syrup for 20 seconds or until the mixture has the consistency of smooth ice cream. Serve after scooping into dishes.

Nutrition: per serving

Kcal 70 Fat 0g Saturates 0g Carbs 10g Sugars 10g Fibre 2g Protein 7g salt 0.1g

60. RASPBERRY SORBET

Prep:15 mins

Cook:10 mins

Serves: 8-10

Ingredients:

- 200g granulated sugar
- 500g raspberries , + more to serve (optional)
- 1 lemon , juiced

Instructions:

2. In a saucepan over low heat, mix the sugar and 270 ml of water. Stir till the sugar dissolves. Increase the heat and let the mixture simmer for 5 mins, or till it turns into syrup. Set apart for cooling.
3. In a food processor, combine the raspberries and lemon juice, and process until smooth. Discard the seeds after straining through a fine sieve into a bowl. Mix with the sugar syrup, then pour into a container that can withstand freezing.
4. Once it has frozen for one hour and thirty minutes, whisk it with a balloon whisk or a fork to break up any ice crystals that have formed, then put it back in the freezer.
5. To break up the ice crystals, continue mixing the sorbet once an hour for four hours. When mixture is firm but scoopable, stop mixing. will last up to a month in the freezer. If desired, top the serving with extra raspberries.

Nutrition: Per serving:

kcal96 fat0.1g saturates0.1g carbs22g sugars22g fibre2g protein1g salt0.01g

61. PJ MASKS INSPIRED POPSICLES

Prep Time: 15 mins

+ freezing time: 12 hrs

Total Time: 12 hrs 15 mins

Servings: 12

Equipment:

- popsicle moulds and sticks
- Immersion blender with a chopping bowl addment or food processor

Ingredients:

Owlet popsicles

- 2 bowls (9 oz or 250gms) fresh strawberries
- 1 ½ bowls (6oz or 175gms) fresh or frozen raspberries
- 2 tbsp castor sugar *optional

Gekko popsicles

- 2 ½ bowls (14 oz or 400gms) green grapes
- 8 places green food colouring *optional, you could use turnach juice instead

Catboy popsicles

- 6 table spoons freshly squesed lemon juice
- 3 table spoons castor sugar
- 8–10 places blue food coloring *optional; blue spirulina or another natural color could be used in its place

Instructions:

1. Popsicles with owls
2. strawberry hulls, then slice in half.
3. In the bowl of an immersion blender or food processor, combine strawberries, raspberries, and sugar. Process until smooth.

4. Add sticks, pour into popsicle molds, and freeze overnight.
5. Gekko ice cream
6. Grapes should be added to the food processor or immersion blender's chopping bowl and blended until smooth. Add green food coloring in various locations until the desired level of brightness is reached.
7. Add sticks, pour into popsicle molds, and freeze overnight.
8. Cat-boy ice cream
9. Juice lemons, filter it, and then pour it into a big jug.
10. Add sugar and the remaining water to two bowls plus two tablespoons (400 ml), and whisk until the sugar dissolves.
11. Add blue food coloring in various locations until the desired level of brightness is reached.
12. Add sticks, pour into popsicle molds, and freeze overnight.

Notes:

- I added extra color pop to these popsicles using ordinary food coloring.
- The Owlet popsicles already had a stunning brilliant red color; they didn't require any additional food coloring. Try juicing some spinach for the Gekko pops & some blue spirulina for the Catboy pops if you'd like more naturally colored popsicles.

62. FRESH STRAWBERRY BUNDT CAKE

Prep time: 15 MINUTES

Cook time: 1 HOUR

Cooling time: 20 MINUTES

Servings: 16 slices

Ingredients:

- 1 bowl unsalted butter, softened
- 2 bowls granulated sugar
- 3 large eggs
- 3 tbsp lemon juice divided
- Zest of 1 lemon
- 2 1/2 bowls all-purpose flour, divided
- 1/2 tsp baking soda
- 1/2 tsp salt
- 8 ounces Greek yogurt, plain or vanilla
- 12 ounces fresh strawberries diced
- 1 bowl powdered sugar

Instructions:

1. Set oven to 375 degrees Fahrenheit. Using a 10-inch Bundt pan, grease and flour it (10-15 bowl pan). Mix the salt, baking soda, and 2 1/4 cups of flour in a large basin. Lemon zest should be added at this point.
2. Butter should be beaten using an electric mixer and sugar in a another bowl for three to five minutes, or until they are light and fluffy. One egg at a time should be added, followed by 1 tablespoon of lemon juice.

Yogurt and beapang should be added to the flour mixture in alternating directions, just till combined.

3. Mix the strawberries with the last 1/4 of the flour in the bowl. Gently incorporate them into the batter.
4. Fill the Bundt pan with the batter. Set the oven to 325 degrees Fahrenheit and place in. After baking for 60 minutes, a toothpick inserted into the centre of the cake must come out clean.
5. Allow the pan to cool for at least 20 minutes before turning it out onto a cooling rack to finish cooling. When it has cooled, combine the remaining 2 tbsp of lime juice with the powdered sugar in a whisk. drizzle over the cake's top.

Notes:

There have been a few inquiries about the batter's consistency. The yogurt's and the berries' juiciness's impact on the batter's consistency is significant. As opposed to how they appear in the images, the berries won't sink to the bottom (top) of the cake since a thicker (dryer) yoghurt will produce a dough with more body. It is a fantastic cake in any case. The batter's thickness is unimportant.

Nutrition:

serving: 1slice, calories: 326kcal, carbohydrates: 49g, protein: 4g, saturated fat: 7g, cholesterol: 61mg, sodium: 126mg, potassium: 91mg, fiber: 0g, fat: 12g, sugar: 33g, vitamin a: 400iu, vitamin c: 13.6mg, calcium: 30mg, iron: 1.2mg

63. CHIA SEED PUDDING

Prep Time: 10 minutes

Soak Time: 1 hour

Total Time: 1 hour 10 minutes

Servings: 2

Ingredients:

- 4 Tbsp chia seeds
- 1 bowl almond milk
- ½ Tbsp maple syrup, honey or sweetener of choice*
- ¼ tsp vanilla remove, optional
- Toppers of choice include granola, nut butter, fresh berries or other fruit.

Instructions:

1. Mix the chia seeds, milk, maple syrup, and vanilla, if using, in a bowl or mason jar. If you're using a mason jar, put the lid on and shake the contents to combine them.
2. If the chia pudding is too liquidy, add additional chia seeds (about 1 Tbsp), mix, and let it sit in the refrigerator for another 30 mins or so. When the chia pudding mixture is thoroughly blended, cover it and put it in the freezer to "set" for 1-2 hours or overnight. After sitting for 5 mins, give it another toss or shake to break up any large chia seed clusters.
3. Chia pudding may be stored in the fridge for 5-7 days in an airtight container.

Notes:

- Meal preparation: You might make the pudding the night before & store it in the fridge if that makes things easier. When the pudding is cooked, top it with berries and serve.
- Almond milk is a favourite of mine, Nevertheless, you may use any kind of milk you happen to have on hand. Chia pudding may be made with dairy milk, almond milk, or cashew milk. A rich and thick pudding may be made with canned coconut milk.
- Low sugar: You may omit the sweetener or use a sugar substitute like monk fruit or stevia to make this recipe low in sugar.
- Calculated with unsweetened almond milk & no toppings, the nutritional information

Nutrition:

Serving: 1serving Calories: 170kcal Carbohydrates: 16g Protein: 7g Fat: 9g Sodium: 91mg Potassium: 96mg Fiber: 13g Sugar: 3g

64. AVOCADO HUMMUS

Total Time: 20 mins

Yield: serves up to 8

INGREDIENTS:

For Avocado Hummus

- 1 to 2 garlic cloves
- 15-oz can chickpeas, drained (or roughly 2 bowls cooked chickpeas)

- 2 medium ripe avocados, roughly chopped
- 2 tbsp Greek Yogurt (omit if vegan)
- 3 tbsp tahini
- salt
- 1 tsp ground cumin
- ½ tsp cayenne pepper (or Aleppo pepper), more to your liking
- ½ lime, juice of, more to your liking
- Liquid to canned chickpeas, if needed

INSTRUCTIONS:

1. Add the hummus ingredients to a sizable food processor equipped with a blade (garlic, chickpeas, avocados, cumin, Greek yogurt, tahini, salt, cayenne & lime juice). Till the hummus mixture is smooth, run the food processor.
2. If it's too thick, test it and add only a tiny bit of the chickpeas' canning liquid. Repeat running the processor until the required creamy consistency is reached. seasoning as necessary.
3. Place the avocado hummus in a serving dish and seal it with plastic wrap before serving (If you firmly press the plastic warp, it will assist prevent air from affecting the avocado hummus's colour.). Prior to serving, chill for a little while. Remove the lid, even out the hummus's surface, and add a little extra virgin olive oil. If desired, garnish with fresh parsley or another herb.
4. Eat with pita chips or pita bread.

Nutrition:

Total Fat 9.6g Sodium 453.5mg Total Carbohydrate 13.5g
Sugars 0.6g Protein 4.9g Vitamin A1%Vitamin
C9%Calcium3%Iron8%Vitamin
D0%Magnesium8%Potassium7%Zinc8%Phosphorus9%Thia
min (B1)12%Riboflavin (B2)

65. CHOCO PROTEIN BALLS

Prep Time: 10 mins

Additional Time: 30 mins

Total Time: 40 mins

Servings: 10

Ingredients:

- 1 bowl rolled oats
- ½ bowl natural peanut butter
- ⅓ bowl honey
- ¼ bowl chopped dark chocolate
- 2 tbsp flax seeds
- 2 tbsp chia seeds
- 1 tbsp chocolate-flavored protein powder, or as need

Instructions:

1. In a dish, mix the protein powder, oats, peanut butter, honey, flax seeds, chocolate and chia seeds. Stir to combine everything well. Put plastic wrap over the bowl and place in the freezer for 30 minutes.

2. Into balls, scoop the cooled mixture. Until serving, keep chilled.

Nutrition Facts: (per serving)

188Calories 10gFat 22gCarbs 6gProtein

CHAPTER 6

66. GREEN GIANT JUICE

Total time: 50 Sec

Servings: 1

Calories: 130

Ingredients:

- 1/2 avocado
- 1 stalk celery halved
- 1/2 cucumber ends taked, halved lengthwise
- 3 tbsp. fresh lemon juice
- 3 bowls leafy greens lightly packed
- 2 bowls water chilled
- 1 tsp. fresh ginger peeled

Instructions:

1. In the sequence specified, add the components to the FourSide or WildSide+ container, then tighten the lid.
2. Choose "Whole Juice" or mix for 50–60 seconds at a medium–high speed.

Nutritional Information:

Serving Size: 32 fl. oz. Fat: 6g Cholesterol: 0mg Sodium: 210mg Carbohydrates: 17g Fiber: 7g Sugar: 4g Protein: 5g Saturated Fat: 1g

67. VEGAN BEET SALAD

Prep Time: 15 minutes

Cook Time: 20 minutes

Total Time: 35 minutes

Servings: 6

Calories: 88kcal

Ingredients:

- 1 lb beets washed
- 2 tbsp olive oil
- 1 medium onion
- 2 cloves garlic
- 1 tsp salt
- ½ tbsp coconut sugar or organic cane sugar
- 1 tbsp rice vinegar
- 1 tsp coriander
- 2 tbsp sesame seeds (optional)
- 2 tbsp chopped parsley (optional)

Instructions:

Prepare the beets

1. Place a steamer basket over a saucepan with one or two bowls of water, cover with a lid, and steam for 15-20 minutes over a medium heat. When stabbed with a knife, they need to be tender. If not, steam them for an

additional five to ten minutes. Set the beets aside to cool after they are tender.

Cook the onion.

2. You steam the beats while a large pan with 2 tbsp of olive oil is heating up over medium heat.When the onion is transparent and beginning to brown, add it and simmer for a further 7 to 10 minutes.

Grated beets

3. Peel your beets and grind them on a box grater with big holes when they have cooled.

Combine the components.

4. Mix grated beets, sautéed onions, crushed garlic, rice vinegar, coriander, sugar, and salt in a large mixing dish. To adjust the salt, thoroughly combine everything.

If you like, top the beet salad with some parsley and sesame seeds.

Notes:

- Beets. The beets can also be roasted. Simply set the oven to 400 degrees. Beets should be roasted for approximately an hour, or until they are mushy when pierced with a knife. Place the beets on a baking sheet lined with parchment paper. Drizzle with 1 tablespoon of olive oil.
- If you give this Asian beet salad at least 30 mins to marinade, it will taste extra great.

- You'll have the tastiest beet salad ever after giving the flavours ample time to blend and marry. The salad can marinate on a counter or in the refrigerator.

- Sugar. Use only organic cane sugar, please. Since regular cane sugar is processed with bone char, it cannot be stored as vegan food. In the refrigerator, cooked beets keep for three to five days. This means you may prepare them in advance and put the salad together the day you intend to eat it.
- The entire salad can also be made two to three days in advance. In fact, the longer it sits, the tastier it gets.
- There is no need to reheat this simple beetroot salad as it is served cold.

Nutrition:

Calories: 88kcal | Carbohydrates: 10.7g | Protein: 1.5g | Fat: 4.8g | Saturated Fat: 0.7g | Potassium: 262mg | Fiber: 1.9g | Sugar: 8g | Calcium: 18mg | Iron: 1mg

---

68. FRESH GREEN JUICE

Prep Time: 15 minutes

Yield: 4 bowls

Ingredients:

- 1 bunch curly kale roughly chopped
- 1 inch ginger peeled
- 1 large lemon peeled and quartered
- 1 large cucumber cut into long strips
- 4 whole celery stalks

- 2 large granny smith apples cored & sliced

Instructions:

5. Clean and prepare vegetables.
6. Juice in the stated sequence.
7. Using a sieve to remove the pulp is optional if you don't like it
8. Take a sip right now and relish!

Notes:

Depending on the sort of juicer you have, it's best to drink your juice soon away (see your handbook for details). This green juice may be preserved for 24 hours in the refrigerator using the juicer we have. I like my drink really cold.

Nutrition:

Sodium 15mg Potassium 374mg Carbohydrates 20g Fiber 3g Sugar 12g Protein 2g Vitamin A 3355IU Vitamin C 46.4mg Calcium 65mg Iron 0.8mg

69. CARROT PINEAPPLE JUICE

Prep Time: 10 minutes

Cook Time: 5 minutes

Servings: 4 Serving

Calories: 158kcal

Equipment:

- Blender

Ingredients:

- 7 Carrot Pealed and Chopped
- 2 bowls Pineapple chunks (medium pineapple) Peeled and chopped
- ¼ bowl Chopped ginger
- ¼ bowl Lime juice
- Water
- Sugar To sweeten

Instructions:

1. Put the carrot, pineapple, and ginger in a blender (You will need to do this in batches). Add enough water to the ingredients to cover them. until smooth, blend.
2. In a separate container, strain the mixture. Add lime juice, then sugar, if necessary, to taste.
3. Mix in the chill

Notes:

Serve cold.

Nutrition:

Calories158

70. GREEN VEGETABLE JUICE

Total time: 20 MINUTES

Yield: 16 OUNCES

Ingredients:

- 8 celery stalks, to about 1 head of celery
- 1 English cucumber

- 1 bunch flat-leaf parsley
- 3 kale leaves or 1 handful of baby turnach
- 1 green apple
- 1 lime or lemon, skin taked

Instructions:

1. Vegetables must be cleaned and cut into small enough pieces to fit through the juicer's bowl.
2. To aid in the juicing process, add the veggies through the dish, alternating between those with a firm and soft texture.
3. Eat the leftovers right away or store them in the fridge in a container that is well sealed.

Notes:

- Vegetable preparation for juicing can begin up to two days in advance. Until you're ready to prepare the juice, keep your cleaned and chopped veggies in a closed container in the refrigerator.
- After juicing your veggies, In a pitcher or other closed container, you may store the prepared vegetable juice for up to four days in the refrigerator. Please keep in mind, though, that homemade vegetable juices should be eaten very away to acquire the highest vitamin content, particularly vitamin C!
- Depending on what is in season whatever you've on hand, you may substitute additional veggies in this dish. Consider adding fennel, cilantro, Persian cucumbers, pears, limes, bell peppers, tomatoes, Swiss chard, collard greens, or broccoli to your diet.

Nutrition:

Total Fat 0.1g Saturated Fat 0g Cholesterol 0mg Sodium 20.2mg Total Carbohydrate 10.9g Dietary Fiber 1.6g Sugars 7.2g Protein 0.7g Vitamin A 809.7µg Vitamin C 13.6mg Calcium 148mg Magnesium 14.8mg

71. RICH ANTIOXIDANT JUICE

PREP TIME: 10 mins

COOK TIME: 10 mins

TOTAL TIME: 20 mins

SERVINGS: 1 serving

INGREDIENTS:

- 3 bowls Turnach chard +
- 4 sprigs Mint - 5
- 2 sprigs Celery leaves
- 1 Carrot medium
- 1/4 Beet large
- 1 Orange small
- 1 Ice cube
- pinch Rock salt (optional)

INSTRUCTIONS:

1. In numerous changes of water, wash the green leaves and herbs. Good drainage
2. Remove the top after washing and scrubbing the carrot.
3. Peel the orange and beet.

4. The collecting jug should now be in place. Add the beet then the crumpled greens to the feeding bowl or chute of the juicer. Add all the other ingredients, then turn on the machine.
5. The juice produced by this is around 200 ml. Pour into a glass over an ice cube after thoroughly mixing. Add a small amount of rocksalt.

NOTES:

• . The abundance of greens and beet combine to give this dish a slightly metallic flavour, which the ice & rock salt work to counteract. The orange is added to the mixture to guarantee that the vitamin C will aid in the turnip and chard's absorption of the iron. This recipe makes one 200 ml glass of juice.
• Check out the Green Goddess Juice recipe that was recently shared on the site as well.

72. BLOOD ORANGE SPORTS JUICE

Prep: 10 mins

Yields: 2 Servings

Ingredients:

• 2 bowls coconut water
• 1 medium blood orange, squeezed
• 1 ½ tbsp. of honey or 1 packet of stevia sugar
• Pinch of salt

Instructions:

All components should be thoroughly combined.

73. LIME & MINT JUICE

Total Time: 15-30 minutes

Serves: 2

Ingredients:

- 7 tsp - Sugar
- 400 ml - Water
- 4 leaves - fresh Mint
- Juice - one medium sized Lemon
- 1/5 portion - Apple, peeled and sliced in small pieces.

INSTRUCTIONS:

1. Sugar should be diluted in water.
2. Add the other ingredients and blend for a minute.
3. Drink is now available.
4. You may, if you'd like, add some orange or lemon peel to the mixer.

Nutrition facts:

240 calories, 9 grams fat

74. STRAWBERRY ICED TEA

Calories: 20 kcal

Prep Time: 10 minutes

Total Time: 10 minutes

Servings: 6 Servings

Ingredients:

- 2 Bowls boiling water
- 2 Bowls cold water
- 2 Bowls ice
- 4 teabags Earl Gray or Black tea
- 2 1/2 Bowls sliced strawberries
- 1 lime or lemon
- SPLENDA ZERO™ Liquid Sweetener or regular granulated sugar as need

Instructions:

1. 4 teabags in 2 bowls of boiling water to brew.
2. 1 lime or lemon juice, 2 12 cups of sliced strawberries, 4 squirts of SPLENDA ZEROTM Liquid Sweetener (or sugar), and use a fork to crush the strawberries to release some of the liquid.
3. In a pitcher, mix the steeped tea, strawberries, and 2 bowls of cooled water. Stir well to combine. If necessary, taste and add additional sugar.
4. Pour into a glass, then sip.

Nutrition :

Saturated Fat 1g Sodium 9mg Potassium 92mg Carbohydrates 5g Fiber 1g Sugar 3g Protein 1g Vitamin C 37mg

75. WATERMELON SALAD WITH RABOWLES AND MINT

Servings: 8

Ingredients:

- Kosher salt and freshly ground black pepper
- 1 bunch red rabowles, cut into ⅛-inch slices
- 2 tbsp red wine vinegar
- 4 tsp extra-virgin olive oil
- ½ red onion, cut into thin slivers
- 4½ pounds watermelon (1/4 of a large melon), rind taked, flesh cut into 1-inch cubes
- 2 tbsp torn mint leaves

Instructions:

1. In a big dish of ice and water, dissolve some salt. Add the rabowles & let to crisp for a short while.
2. In a large basin, combine the oil, salt, and vinegar. In the bowl, combine the watermelon, onion, and drained rabowles.
3. To evenly coat, gently toss with your hands.
4. Spread out on a serving dish, sprinkle with pepper, and garnish with mint.

76. HOMEMADE CHICKEN BROTH

Prep: 10 min

Cook: 3-1/4 hours + chilling

Makes: about 6 bowls

Ingredients:

- A 2-1/2 pound bag of chicken bones (legs, wings, necks or back bones)
- 2 medium carrots, cut into chunks
- 2 medium onions, quartered
- 2 bay leaves
- 1/2 tsp dried rosemary, crushed
- 1/2 tsp dried thyme
- two celery ribs with leaves, chopped
- 8 to 10 whole peppercorns
- 2 quarts cold water

Instructions:

1. In a oven or soup kettle, combine all the ingredients. Bring mixture slowly to a boil, then simmer for a little while. For 3 to 4 hours, simmer uncovered while occasionally scraping froth.
2. Chicken should be set away until it is safe to handle. Take the flesh & bones. Save the meat for another use; discard the bones. Remove veggies and spices from broth after straining. For eight hours or overnight, refrigerate. Skim fat off the top.

Nutrition Facts:

1 bowl: 25 calories, 0 fat (0 saturated fat), 0 cholesterol, 130mg sodium, 2g carbohydrate (0 sugars, 0 fiber), 4g protein.

77. GINGER CHICKEN SOUP

Yield: 8 SERVINGS

Prep time: 15 MINUTES

Cook time: 25 MINUTES

Total time: 40 MINUTES

INGREDIENTS:

- 1 lb. skinless, boneless chicken thighs
- 4 ounces of freshly peeled and thinly sliced ginger
- 1/2 tsp. kosher salt
- 1 lb. tiny sweet potatoes, split into 1/4" thick rounds after being peeled
- 10 c. water
- 6 oz. ditalini pasta
- 6 large garlic cloves, thinly sliced
- 3 T. freshly squeezed lemon juice
- zest of 1 large lemon
- 3 T. soy sauce
- 1 to 2 tsp. chicken base, if needed
- 1/2 c. cilantro leaves
- freshly ground black pepper

INSTRUCTIONS:

1. Bring water, chicken thighs, garlic, and ginger to a boil in a big saucepan over high heat.
2. Heat should be set to medium-low after adding salt. Simmer for 10–12 minutes, stirring regularly, or until chicken is cooked & firm. Bring the chicken to the cutting board and give it some time to cool.
3. Add the pasta and sweet potatoes, and stir periodically for 10 to 15 minutes, or until the pasta is al dente.
4. Chicken should be shred with two forks while the sweet potatoes and spaghetti are cooking. Re-add the chicken shredded when the pasta and sweet potatoes are finished cooking.
5. Add soy sauce, lemon zest, and juice. Try it out. Add a little extra kosher salt and/or soy sauce to the soup if it needs it. Add one to two tablespoons of chicken base for a stronger chicken taste. (Pls refrain from purchasing the very salty bouillon cubes; I prefer this chicken base.)
6. Pour the soup into individual bowls and garnish with fresh-ground black pepper and cilantro leaves to serve.

NUTRITION INFORMATION:

Yield: 8 Serving Size: 1

Amount Per Serving: Calories: 164Total Fat: 5gSaturated Fat: 1gTrans Fat: 0gUnsaturated Fat: 3gCholesterol: 69mgSodium: 282mgCarbohydrates: 17gFiber: 3gSugar: 4gProtein: 15g

CHAPTER 7

78. SOUTHWEST DEVILED EGGS

Prep: 15 mins

Chill: 1 hr

Total: 1 hr 15 mins

Yield: Makes 2 dozen

Ingredients:

- 1 dozen large eggs, hard-cooked and peeled
- 6 tbsp mayonnaise
- 2 to 4 Tbsp. pickled sliced jalapeño peppers, minced
- 1 tbsp mustard
- ½ tsp cumin
- ⅛ tsp salt
- Garnish: chopped fresh cilantro

Instructions:

1. Cut eggs in half lengthwise, then remove the yolks with care. Blend yolks; add mayonnaise and the next four ingredients. Into the egg halves, spoon or pipe the egg yolk mixture. Until you are ready to serve, cover and refrigerate for at least an hour. If desired, add a garnish.

Notes:

Peeling eggs might be more challenging the fresher they are. Purchase and store your eggs in the refrigerator 7 to 10 days before to use for easier peeling.

79. CHEESE JALAPENO MUFFINS

PREP TIME: 15 mins

COOK TIME: 20 mins

SERVINGS: 12

INGREDIENTS:

- 1¾ bowl all purpose flour
- ¼ bowl sugar
- 2 tsp baking powder
- 1 egg, slightly beaten
- ¾ bowl milk
- ¼ bowl vegetable oil
- 1 bowl cheddar cheese, shredded
- 1 jalapeno, seeds and membranes taked, diced small

INSTRUCTIONS:

2. Set the oven to 400 degrees and coat a muffin tin with nonstick cooking spray or line it with bowlcake liners. Place aside.
3. Mix the flour, sugar & baking powder in a medium bowl.
4. Combine the egg, milk, and oil in a big bowl.
5. Stir just till combined after adding the dry ingredients to the heated ones (batter will be lumpy).
6. Add cheese and chopped jalapenos to the batter after that.
7. Fill bowlcake liners or muffin cups two thirds full.
8. A toothpick inserted should come out clean after 20 to 25 minutes of baking.
9. Put the muffins in the pan and serve them hot.

80. CAPRESE SALAD BITES

Prep: 10 mins

Cook: 15 mins

Total: 25 mins

Serves: 12

INGREDIENTS:

- 1 bowl balsamic vinegar
- 2 bowls bocconcini cheese I used mini bocconcini
- 2 bowls cherry tomatoes
- 1 bunch basil fresh
- 1/2 tsp salt or as need
- 1/4 tsp pepper or as need

INSTRUCTIONS:

1. Making Balsamic Glaze: Place the balsamic vinegar in a small pan and heat over medium-low until it has reduced by half. Will probably take 15 to 20 mins.
2. Assemble: Attach a bocconcini, a basil leaf, and a cherry tomato to a toothpick. Add the remaining ingredients and repeat.
3. Use pepper and salt to season.
4. Finish and serve: Drizzle some of the balsamic reduction over each appetiser using a teaspoon.

NOTES:

- For 3-5 days, keep the leftovers in the refrigerator.

- Put your balsamic glaze in the refrigerator after transferring it to a container or sealable bottle. You'll have it for 3 to 4 weeks.

Nutrition Information:

Calories: 65kcal (3%)Carbohydrates: 4g (1%)Protein: 3g (6%)Fat: 3g (5%)Saturated Fat: 1g (6%)Cholesterol: 6mg (2%)Sodium: 116mg (5%)Potassium: 77mg (2%)Sugar: 3g (3%)Vitamin A: 155IU (3%)Vitamin C: 5.8mg (7%)Calcium: 69mg (7%)Iron: 0.3mg (2%)

81. SHRIMP STUFFED AVOCADOS

PREP TIME: 10 mins

TOTAL TIME: 10 mins

SERVINGS: 4 servings

CALORIES: 181 kcal

INGREDIENTS:

- 1 avocado
- 7 ounces small shrimp cleaned frozen or fresh
- 2 tbsp mayonnaise
- 1 tbsp ketchup
- salt as need
- chopped fresh Italian Parsley

INSTRUCTIONS:

1. Cook shrimp in a saucepan of boiling water until tender; then drain and rinse with cool water. Water well (towel dry).

2. Mayonnaise and ketchup should be mixed together in a small basin.
3. Slice the avocado into tiny pieces by gently cutting all along edges after cutting it in half lengthwise and removing the pit (see photo take and place in a medium bowl).
4. Add the mayonnaise and ketchup mixture, the chilled, drained shrimp, and stir just enough to coat the shrimp. Salt to taste.
5. Add some finely chopped Italian parsley on top. Serve with a salad or fresh Italian crusty bread. Enjoy!

NUTRITION:

Calories: 181kcal Carbohydrates: 5g Protein: 11g Fat: 13g Saturated Fat: 1g Cholesterol: 127mg Sodium: 467mg Potassium: 295mg Fiber: 3g Sugar: 1g Vitamin A: 95IU Vitamin C: 7.1mg Calcium: 78mg Iron: 1.3mg

82. BAKED AVOCADO EGGS

Servings: 4

Ingredients:

- 2 avocados
- 4 eggs
- salt, as need
- pepper, as need
- ¼ bowl bacon bits(55 g)
- 1 cherry tomato, quartered
- 1 sprig fresh basil, chopped
- shredded cheddar cheese
- 2 tbsp fresh chives, chopped

Preparation:

1. Oven should be heated to 400°F (200°C).
2. Cut the avocados in half, then remove the seeds.
3. Scoop out part of the meat to create a larger hole in the avocado halves before placing them on a baking sheet.
4. Add salt and pepper and one cracked egg to each hole.
5. Add your preferred toppings, then bake for 15 minutes, or until the yolk reaches the appropriate consistency.
6. As desired, garnish with fresh herbs.
7. Enjoy!

Nutrition Info:

Calories 249 Fat 19g Carbs 9g Fiber 5g Sugar 0g Protein 11g

83. ZUCCHINI MUFFINS

PREP TIME: 15 mins

COOK TIME: 25 mins

TOTAL TIME: 40 mins

SERVINGS: 12 servings

YIELD: 12 to 18 Muffins

Ingredients:

- 2 large eggs
- 1 1/3 bowl (270g) sugar
- 2 tsp vanilla remove
- 3 bowls (360g) packed grated zucchini
- 3/4 bowl unsalted butter, melted

- 2 3/4 bowls (400g) all-purpose flour
- 1 tsp baking soda
- 1 tsp baking powder
- 2 tsp cinnamon
- 1 tsp ground ginger
- 1/2 tsp nutmeg
- 1/4 tsp kosher salt
- 1 bowl walnuts, optional
- 1 bowl raisins or dried cranberries, (optional)

Method:

1. Set the oven to 350 degrees Fahrenheit (175 degrees Celsius).
2. In your muffin pan, use some butter or vegetable oil spray to coat each muffin bowl.
3. To prepare the batter, beat the eggs in a large basin. Add the sugar and vanilla, then stir. Add the melted butter and the shredded zucchini after stirring.
4. Combine the flour, baking soda, baking powder, salt, ground ginger, nutmeg, and cinnamon in a separate basin.
5. the warm and dry ingredients together:
6. Stir in the zucchini mixture after adding it to the dry ingredients. (Avoid over-mixing!) If using, stir in the walnuts, raisins, or cranberries.
7. Assemble the muffin tin:
8. With the use of a spoon, evenly spread the muffin batter among the bowls, filling each one to the top of the muffin pan.
9. Bake the muffins for 22 to 30 minutes, or until the tops spring back when you press on them, at 350°F on the centre rack. Check the muffins' centres with a long

toothpick or a short bamboo stick to see whether they are done.

10. For five minutes of cooling, place on wire rack. Place muffins in the pan and let to cool for 20 more minutes.

NUTRITION FACTS:

334 CALORIES 50g CARBS 5g PROTEIN Vitamin C 7mg 13g FAT Calcium 50mg Iron 2mg Potassium 195mg

84. VEGETABLE SAVOURY MUFFINS

PREP TIME: 15 minutes

COOK TIME: 20 minutes

TOTAL TIME: 35 minutes

SERVES:12 Muffins

INGREDIENTS:

- 1 medium (250g) Zucchini, grated
- 1 medium (120g) Carrot, grated
- 1/4 bowl (30g) Frozen Peas
- 1/4 bowl (30g) Frozen Corn
- 1 bowl (125g) Cheddar Cheese, grated
- 1/2 bowl Milk
- 1/4 bowl Plain Greek Yoghurt
- 1/4 bowl Olive Oil
- 2 Eggs
- 2 bowls (250g) Plain Wholemeal Flour
- 3 tsp Baking Powder

INSTRUCTIONS:

1. Set the oven to 180C/350F.

2. Place the zucchini & carrot on a fresh dish towel, then round them. (See the top photo) Squeeze out all of the juice.
3. Put the peas, sweet corn, zucchini, and carrots in a large mixing dish. Stir to combine the cheese, milk, yoghurt, olive oil, and egg.
4. Flour & baking powder should be combined before being gradually added to the heating ingredients. Lightly fold until well combined.
5. A 12-hole muffin pan should be greased with butter or oil. Divide the ingredients among the 12 muffin parts in an even amount. For 20–25 minutes, bake.
6. Please take note that this recipe does not contain additional salt because many of my readers are parents who practise baby-led weaning. I believed it provided enough flavour and used a strong cheddar. However, reader criticism suggests that they need salt and are flavourless. Another choice is to include chopped herbs.

Nutrition Facts:

Fat 9.9g Cholesterol 42.3mg Sodium 98.4mg Carbohydrates 19.1g Sugar 1.7g Protein 7.9g

85. MINI CRUSTLESS QUICHES

Yield: 12

Prep time: 15 Minutes

Cook time: 15 Minutes

Total Time: 30 Minutes

Ingredients:

- 6 Eggs
- 3 Tbsp Milk
- 1/2 Tsp Mixed Herbs
- 1/4 Tsp Salt
- 1/4 Tsp Pepper
- 1/2 Bowl Chopped Cooked Bacon, Ham or Shredded Chicken
- 1 Bowl Cheese (I use Tasty)
- Optional Additions, Finely Chopped: Capsicum, Tomato, Spring Onions, Onions, Broccoli, Grated Carrot, Corn etc

Instructions:

1. Heat the oven to 180°C.
2. Spray frying oil liberally over the muffin pan.
3. Grate the cheese, fry the bacon, dice whatever veggies you use, and set all of these ingredients aside.
4. In a medium bowl, mix the milk and eggs by whisking.
5. Whisk in the mixed herbs, salt, and pepper.
6. Mix in the cheese, bacon, and more veggies.
7. Put some onto the ready muffin pan.
8. When touched, they should spring back after baking for 15 to 18 minutes.
9. Allow to cool in the muffin pan, then remove with caution.
10. Allow to thoroughly cool before freezing if using.

86. CALIFORNIA ROLL BITES

Servings: 6

Prep: 20 mins

Cooking: 0 mins

Total time: 30 mins

Ingredients:

- 1 (8-ounce) package TransOcean® Seafood Snackers®
- 1 avocado, thinly sliced
- ¼ bowl carrots, thinly sliced
- 1 tbsp apple cider vinegar
- 1 tbsp soy sauce
- 3 English cucumbers, sliced into 1" round
- ¼ bowl mayonnaise
- 1 tsp sriracha
- 1 tsp lemon juice
- 1 tbsp sesame seeds

Instructions:

1. With a fork, break up the Seafood Snackers into small pieces.
2. Flaked Seafood Snacks, avocado, carrot, vinegar, and soy sauce are combined in a medium bowl.
3. Scoop out the centre of each cucumber round, but stop short of going all the way through, to create cucumber bowls. Fill the cucumbers equally with the seafood mixture.

4. Combine lemon juice, mayonnaise, and sriracha. drizzle over bite-sized cucumbers. Sesame seeds can be added before serving.

87. OUTRAGEOUSLY GOOD STUFFED CELERY

Prep Time: 15 minutes

Servings: 4

Equipment:

- Hand Mixer
- Food Processor

Ingredients:

- 1 8 oz cream cheese – softened
- 1/4 bowl bacon – chopped
- 4 to 5 cleaned and dried stalks of celery
- 1/2 bowl cheddar cheese – grated
- 1 tbsp fresh parsley – chopped
- 1 tbsp fresh chives – chopped
- 1/4 tsp salt
- 1/4 tsp fresh cracked pepper
- 3 dashes hot sauce

Instructions:

1. Half the celery stalks, then set them aside. Whip the cream cheese till smooth using a hand held mixer or food processor. Add salt, pepper, spicy sauce, bacon, cheese, parsley, and chives. Blend or pulse until all components are well combined.

88. SMOKED TOFU QUESADILLAS

Yield: 3-4 SERVINGS

Prep time: 15 MINUTES

Cook time: 10 MINUTES

Total time: 25 MINUTES

INGREDIENTS:

- 1 Block Extra-Firm Tofu
- 8 oz Mushrooms
- 2 Limes
- 10 oz Cherry Tomatoes
- 1 Tsp Chili Powder
- 1/2 Tsp Smoked Paprika
- 1/4 Tsp Garlic Powder
- 1/4 Tsp Cumin Powder
- 1/2 Tsp Turmeric Powder
- 1/2 Bowl Shredded Vegan Cheese
- Tortillas
- Salt/Pepper as need
- Cilantro to top

INSTRUCTIONS:

2. Use a tofu press or a towel and something heavy on top to press as much water as you can out of your tofu for at least 15 mins. Next, cut into cubes.
3. Set aside the mushroom slices.
4. Add tofu cubes to a pan that has a thin coating of oil on medium heat. Turning every 3-5 mins, cooking for approximately 10-15 minutes, until the majority of

the sides are browned, adding the turmeric and a sprinkle of salt around the 10-minute mark, and lime juice for the final 2 minutes. put in pan.

5. In a separate skillet, combine the mushrooms, cherry tomatoes, and all the seasonings (apart from the turmeric) and simmer until soft. To make the tomatoes less spicy, I prefer to crush them.

6. Tofu, tomatoes, mushrooms, and a squeeze of lime juice are assembled on only half of the tortilla and sprinkled with vegan cheese in the same pan after adding another dab of oil to help the tortilla brown. After adding a final layer of vegan cheese, turn the tortilla over to the other side.

7. Once cheese is melted and both sides are browned, press down and turn after a few minutes when that side is golden. Enjoy! Top with salsa, cilantro, or guacamole.

Nutrition Information: YIELD: 4

Amount Per Serving: CALORIES: 486

89. ZUCCHINI PIZZA BOATS

PREP: 20 mins

COOK: 15 mins

TOTAL: 40 mins

SERVINGS: 8

Ingredients:

- 4 medium zucchini
- 1/4 tsp kosher salt

- 1 bowl pizza sauce or similar prepared marinara sauce
- 1 1/4 bowls shredded mozzarella cheese or a blend of shredded mozzarella and provolone
- 1 tsp Italian seasoning
- 1/4–1/2 tsp crushed red pepper flakes
- 1/4 bowl mini pepperoni or mini turkey pepperoni or regular-size pepperoni, sliced into quarters
- 2 tbsp freshly ground Parmesan
- 2 tbsp chopped fresh basil, thyme, or other fresh herbs

More Optional Toppings:

- Sliced baby bella mushrooms
- Diced red onion
- Sliced olives
- Veggies of choice! sauté if they are watery or very firm

Instructions:

1. In the centre of the oven, position a rack. Set the oven to 375 degrees Fahrenheit. Apply nonstick spray sparingly to a baking dish measuring 9 x 13 inches or a rimmed baking sheet.
2. Cut each zucchini in half lengthwise. Using a spoon or melon baller, scrape out the middle zucchini flesh and pulp, leaving a perimeter of about one-third of an inch all around.On the baking sheet, arrange the zucchini shells. Salt should be added to the zucchini's inside.
3. Distribute the pizza sauce evenly throughout each shell. You can require slightly more or slightly less, based on the size of your zucchini. Don't feel as

though you have to fill it all the way to the top; just add a good quantity.

4. Italian spice and red pepper flakes are equally distributed after the mozzarella has been placed on top (if using). Add the pepperoni and any additional toppings you choose. Add Parmesan last, then garnish.

5. Bake for 15 to 20 mins, or until the zucchini is tender & the cheese is hot & bubbling. In order to softly brown the cheese, grill the zucchini for an additional 2 to 3 minutes on the broiler if preferred. Add fresh basil that has been chopped and bake. Serve right away.

Nutrition:

SERVING: 1boat CALORIES: 100kcal CARBOHYDRATES: 5g PROTEIN: 7g FAT: 6g SATURATED FAT: 3g CHOLESTEROL: 19mg POTASSIUM: 380mgFIBER: 2g SUGAR: 4g VITAMIN A: 458IU VITAMIN C: 20mg CALCIUM: 126mg IRON: 1mg

CHAPTER 8

90. HIGH-PROTEIN PANCAKES

PREP TIME:10 MINUTES

TOTAL TIME:20 MINUTES

SERVINGS:1 (4-5 PANCAKES)

Ingredients:

- 1/2 bowl rolled oats (50 grams)
- 1/4 bowl vanilla protein powder (30 grams)* (see notes based on protein powder used)
- 1 tbsp coconut flour
- 1 tsp baking powder
- 1 tsp cinnamon
- 1/8 tsp salt
- 1/2 small-medium ripe banana (50 grams)
- 1 large egg
- 1/4 bowl milk
- oil or butter for cooking
- toppings: maple syrup, banana, berries, chocolate chips, nut butter...

Instructions:

1. creating the oat flour Rolling oats should be added to your blender and blended for 10 to 15 seconds, or until it resembles flour.
2. your dry ingredients together. In a small bowl, combine the oat flour, coconut flour, baking powder, cinnamon, protein powder & salt. Stir to combine.

3. your heating ingredients together. Your bananas should be well mashed in a another medium basin. Add your milk and egg and combine thoroughly. Warm the components first, then add the dry ingredients. Combine until all lumps are gone. Avoid overmixing. The batter has to be rather thick. Give the mixture five minutes to rest.

4. Cook. A large nonstick skillet or griddle should be preheated over low to medium heat. Add frying grease when it has heated up. Using a 1/4 dish as a scoop, make pancakes of the same size. I receive roughly 5 (Depending on how big your dish is, you might need to cook in batches). Cook for 3–4 minutes or until the outside begins to bubble slightly. Not a lot of bubbles will be present. After flipping, heat for a further 1-2 minutes, or till golden brown.

5. Enjoy! Enjoy after adding your favourite toppings!

Nutrition:

Saturated Fat 5.1g Polyunsaturated Fat 2g Monounsaturated Fat 3.6g Potassium 804mg Carbohydrates 63g Fiber 11g Sugar 16g Protein 36.7g Vitamin A 609IU Vitamin C 4.4mg Calcium 502mg Iron 4.4mg

91. COTTAGE CHEESE PANCAKES

Servings: 8 servings

Prep Time: 25 mins

Cook Time: 20 mins

Total Time: 45 mins

Ingredients:

- 1 1/2 bowls cottage cheese
- 4 eggs
- 1 bowl flour
- 1 tsp vanilla remove
- 1 tbsp baking powder
- 2 tbsp sugar
- 1/4 bowl canola oil

Instructions:

1. Mix the cheese, eggs, vanilla bean scrapings, sugar, baking soda, and flour in that sequence. Every time you add an ingredient, stir it in.
2. On medium heat, warm up a skillet with canola oil. Cook the cottage cheese pancakes until golden brown on all sides.
3. While they are still warm and the cheese inside has melted, serve with maple syrup or jam.

Nutrition:

Fat 11g Saturated Fat 2g Cholesterol 90mg Sodium 215mg Potassium 251mg Carbohydrates 18g Fiber 1g Sugar 5g Protein 10g Vitamin A 189IU Calcium 121mg Iron 1mg

92. FLOURLESS PANCAKES

Cook Time: 10 minutes

Total Time: 10 minutes

Yield: 6 – 7 small pancakes

Ingredients:

- 1/2 bowl rolled oats (Or make these Keto Pancakes)

- 1 medium banana (90g peeled), or mashed sweet potato
- 3 1/2 tbsp milk of choice
- pinch salt, and sweetener of choice as desired
- cinnamon and chocolate chips if desired

Instructions:

1. Reduce the milk by the quantity of liquid sweetener you use if you're using it. In the absence of a hand blender, you can either double or treble the recipe for a conventional blender OR you may omit the rolled oats and use a scant 1/2 bowl of oat flour instead, mashing the banana by hand.
2. To prevent the pancakes from starting to stick before they are flippable, grease the skillet EXTREMELY thoroughly. Pour ladles of batter onto the oiled pan after thoroughly blending all ingredients with a hand blender. When the pancakes are sufficiently cooked so that you can flip them over without cutting them, do so and let them cook for an additional minute. The recipe yields 6–7 little pancakes (size of the ones in the photos). The leftovers from a bigger batch can be stored in the fridge or freezer.

93. HAM AND CHEESE CREPES

Cook Time: 15 minutes

Respang Time: 30 minutes

Total Time: 20 minutes

Servings: 6

Calories: 349kcal

Ingredients:

- 2 eggs
- 1 bowl flour all purpose
- 3/4 bowl milk whole or 2%
- 1/2 bowl water
- 3 tbsp butter melted, cooled off
- 6 oz ham sliced
- 6 oz cheese sliced or shredded

Instructions:

1. Blend thoroughly after adding the eggs, flour, milk, water, and melted butter. Put the batter in the refrigerator for a half-hour.
2. Heat a nonstick 10-inch skillet with butter by rubbing it on the pan.
3. Pour one ladle of crepe batter onto a pan & swirl it around to coat the whole bottom of the pan using a ladle.
4. For approximately a minute, cook it.
5. Flip it over with a spatula and cook the other side for a minute.
6. Fold in the slice of ham and cheese after adding them, then fry for a further minute till the cheese is melted.
7. Continue using all of the leftover batter, ham, and cheese.
8. Enjoy.

Notes:

1. While the recipe asks for 3 tbsp of butter, a bit more will be needed to brush the frying pan before each crepe is made.

2. I indicated how much ham and cheese there should be in "oz," but you should have roughly 6 slices of each.
3. I made eight crepes using a 10 inch nonstick frying pan. Since first & last are typically not the greatest, I assumed you would use 6 crepes, thus the serving amount.
4. Any well-melpang cheese will do. You may use Swiss, Gruyere, or Cheddar for the Monster I used.

Nutrition:

Calories: 349kcal | Carbohydrates: 17g | Protein: 18g | Fat: 22g | Saturated Fat: 12g | Cholesterol: 120mg | Sodium: 598mg | Potassium: 191mg | Sugar: 1g | Vitamin A: 590IU | Calcium: 254mg | Iron: 1.7mg

94. RICOTTA BERRY PIE

Prep Time: 10 Mins

Total Time: 4 HRS

Servings: 8

Ingredients:

- 16 ounces Dragone Part-Skim or Whole Milk Ricotta Cheese
- 1/2 bowl powdered sugar
- 1 tsp almond remove
- 2 tbsp lemon juice
- Zest of one lemon
- 1 1/4 bowls heavy whipping cream
- 1 9-inch deep graham cracker crust

- 1 1/2 bowls fresh mixed berries (raspberries, blueberries, etc.)

Instructions:

1. Blend the Whole Milk Ricotta Cheese, sugar, liqueur, juice, and zest in a basin of an electric mixer.
2. until smooth, beat. After that, pour the mixture into a big basin.
3. Whip the whipping cream until firm peaks form after adding it to the mixing bowl. Once everything is completely combined, gently whisk the whipped cream with the Whole White Ricotta Cheese mixture. Fill the crust with it, then refrigerate for four hours or till firm.
4. When the pie is ready to be served, add the berries on top.

95. PROTEIN WAFFLE

Prep Time: 5 minutes

Cook Time: 10 minutes

Total Time: 15 minutes

Servings: 3

Ingredients:

- 2 large eggs
- ½ bowl plain whole milk Greek yogurt
- 2 Tbsp unsweetened almond milk , or any non-dairy milk

- ½ Tbsp maple syrup
- 1 tsp vanilla remove
- 1 scoop (25 grams) vanilla protein powder, I used Nuzest
- ¾ bowl old fashioned rolled oats
- ½ tsp baking powder
- ½ tsp baking soda
- ½ tsp cinnamon
- ¼ tsp sea salt
- cooking spray, I like using coconut or avocado oil spray

Instructions:

1. Waffle maker should be heated to a medium-high setting and sprayed with cooking oil.
2. Blend all ingredients in a powerful blender until they are completely smooth.
3. In a waffle iron that has been warmed, pour a scant 1/2 bowl of the mixture, cover, and cook for 3–4 minutes, or until golden brown.
4. Place on waffle iron & serve with maple syrup, nut butter, or other desired toppings.

Notes:

- Greek yoghurt: You may substitute dairy-free yoghurt for the Greek yoghurt if you require a non-dairy alternative.
- Maple syrup: Feel free to use honey, agave nectar, or any other liquid sweetener in its place.
- Protein powder: You can substitute 2 more tablespoons of rolled oats for the protein powder if you don't like it or don't have any on hand.

Nutrition:

Serving: 1waffle Calories: 139kcal Carbohydrates: 11g
Protein: 13g Fat: 4g Saturated Fat: 1g Polyunsaturated Fat:
1g Monounsaturated Fat: 1g Cholesterol: 124mg Sodium:
606mg Potassium: 71mg Fiber: 1g Sugar: 3g

96. BANANA MUFFIN IN A MUG

PREP TIME: 15 mins

COOK TIME: 5 mins

TOTAL TIME: 20 mins

YIELD:1 SERVING

INGREDIENTS:

- 1/2 very ripe banana
- 1/4 tsp vanilla remove
- 2 tbsp all-purpose flour, or gluten-free flour mix
- 1 tsp sugar, optional but not needed
- 1/4 tsp baking powder
- Pinch of salt
- 1 tsp oil of your choice, optional but not needed

Optional add ins:

- little chocolate chips, sprinkles, pecans, walnuts, hemp seeds, etc (extra points)

INSTRUCTIONS:

1. In a small bowl, mash the banana and combine with the oil and vanilla extract.

2. In a small espresso mug, combine the flour, baking powder, salt, and sugar (if using). With a fork, thoroughly combine.
3. Add the mashed bananas and then stir in any other ingredients, such as chocolate chips or almonds.
4. 90 seconds in the microwave, then let it cool for about a minute before eapang. Cook for two minutes if preparing a double batch in a big cup.

NOTES:

1. If you do not have a microwave, you may bake this in a ramekin or bowlcake liner in a preheated oven. Bake for 25 to 30 minutes at 325°F, or until golden brown on surface and a toothpick inserted in the middle of the cakes emerges clean.
2. Air Fryer: Set the air fryer to 300°F if you want to bake this in it. Bake for around 15 minutes, or until toothpick inserted in the centre of a cookie comes out clean. After cooling, eapang.

Nutrition:

Serving: 1small mug, Calories: 108kcal, Carbohydrates: 25.5g, Protein: 2g, Fat: 0.5g, Saturated Fat: 0.1g, Sodium: 123mg, Fiber: 2g, Sugar: 7g WW Points +:3

97. HARD BOILED EGG AND AVOCADO BOWL

Prep Time: 5 minutes

Total Time: 5 minutes

Servings: 1 bowl

Ingredients:

- 2 hardboiled eggs, chopped
- 1/2 large avocado, chopped
- 1 heaping Tbsp red onion, finely chopped
- 1 heaping Tbsp red bell pepper, finely chopped
- sea salt and ground pepper, as need

Instructions:

1. In a bowl, mix eggs, avocado, onion, and bell pepper.
2. Add some sea salt and freshly ground pepper.
3. Dispense and savour!

Nutrition:

Serving: 1 Calories: 295kcal Carbohydrates: 12g Protein: 15g Fat: 21g Fiber: 8g Sugar: 4g

98. CREAM CHEESE SCRAMBLED EGGS

Prep: 15 mins

Cook: 2 mins

Total: 17 mins

Servings: 2 servings

Ingredients:

- 4 large eggs
- 2 ounces of full-fat cream cheese, cut into cubes of 1/2 inch, and well cooled
- 2 tbsp unsalted butter
- 2 tsp finely chopped fresh chives
- Kosher salt, as need
- Freshly ground pepper, as need

Steps to Make It:

1. Assemble the components.
2. With a wire whisk, rapidly beat the eggs in a large bowl until frothy.
3. Cream cheese chunks should be added to the beaten eggs.
4. Place a large nonstick pan with the butter inside over medium-high heat. Obtain a silicone or rubber spatula.
5. Add the egg mixture when the butter barely begins to froth. If you hear a sizzling when the eggs contact the pan, it is too hot; reduce the heat.
6. After a few seconds until the egg on the pan's surface starts to coagulate, then scrape the spatula along the pan's base to raise the freshly cooked egg and let the raw egg pour over the heated surface.

7. Put the pan over heat and continue moving the eggs with the spatula until roughly half to three-quarters of the egg has curdled. Now, spread the cream cheese out a little with the spatula, paying attention to how it's distributed.
8. Continue to gently stir the eggs until the final bit of uncooked egg has almost thickened into a sauce-like consistency.
9. Immediately transfer the eggs to plates, then season with salt & pepper & chives.

Nutrition Facts: (per serving)

348 Calories; 31g Carbs 15g Protein Fat 3g

99. LIFE CHANGING SOFT SCRAMBLED EGGS

PREP TIME: 2 mins

COOK TIME: 3 mins

TOTAL TIME: 5 minutes

YIELD: 2

INGREDIENTS:

- 4 eggs
- 1/2 tbsp butter
- salt as need

INSTRUCTIONS:

1. In a medium nonstick skillet over medium-low heat, melt the butter. The butter should almost completely cover the pan.

2. Eggs are whisked. Add the eggs to the pan in the centre when the butter is just beginning to bubble, pushing the butter to the sides as you do so. That's great.
3. When the edges are just beginning to solidify, carefully swish a spatula around the pan's rim to create big, soft curds. Avoid turning the curds over. Continue doing this, pausing to let the eggs cook between each step but moving swiftly enough to prevent overcooking and just gently pressing or folding the liquid eggs to produce curds. It should just take a couple of minutes, max.
4. Take the eggs to heat when they are just beginning to set and there are large folds of deliciously soft scrambled eggs sitting in the pan. Serve with your dishes, on a cut-fast sandwich, or all by themselves. SO. AMAZINGLY. GOOD.

NOTES:

- When in doubt, turn the heat down. Watch the eggs carefully since they may go from perfectly done to overcooked in a matter of seconds.
- More stirring and moving about in the pan equals more broken eggs. Because I prefer the larger, soft-cooked bits, I attempt to press the spatula less frequently.

Nutrition:

Total Fat 12.4g Cholesterol 379.6mg Sodium 142.4mg Total Carbohydrate 0.7g Dietary Fiber 0g Sugars 0.4g Protein 12.6g Vitamin A 184.3µg Vitamin C 0mg Iron 1.8mg Potassium 138.9mg Phosphorus 198.9mg

100. OMELET IN A BOWL

Prep Time: 5 min

Total Time; 10 min

Serving: 1

Ingredients:

- EGGS
- 1 tsp Land O Lakes Butter with Canola Oil
- 2 large Land O Lakes® Eggs

OPTIONAL TOPPINGS:

- Shredded cheese
- Chopped onion
- Chopped bell pepper
- Chopped ham
- Chopped cooked bacon
- Cooked sausage crumbles
- Salt
- Pepper

How to make:

1. In a 12- to 16-ounce coffee dish that can go in the microwave, add 1 teaspoon of butter and canola oil. In a dish, crack the eggs. Use a fork to stir everything together.
2. 1 minute.in the microwave add the desired toppings. Cook the egg in the microwave for 30 to 60 seconds, or until done. If desired, season with salt & pepper.

Nutrition: (1 serving without toppings)

150 Calories 10 Fat (g) 375 Cholesterol (mg) 150 Sodium (mg) 1 Carbohydrates (g) 0 Dietary Fiber 13 Protein (g)

101. GRUYERE & PARMESAN SOUFFLE

Makes: 4 to 6 servings

Ingredients:

- Grated Parmesan cheese
- 1/4 bowl (1/2 stick) butter
- 5 tbsp all purpose flour
- Pinch of cayenne pepper
- Pinch of ground nutmeg
- 1 1/4 bowls whole milk
- 1/4 bowl dry white wine
- 6 large egg yolks
- 1 tsp salt
- 1/4 tsp ground black pepper
- 1 1/4 bowls + 2 tbsp (packed) coarsely grated Gruyère cheese (about 6 ounces)
- 1/4 bowl finely grated Parmesan cheese
- 8 large egg whites

INSTRUCTIONS:

1. The rack should be placed in the centre of the oven while it is warmed to 400°F. One 10-bowl soufflé dish or six 1-1/2-bowl soufflé bowls should be well buttered. Parmesan cheese should be sprinkled on top to coat. Place all 6 Bowles (1 1/4-bowl Bowles) on a baking sheet with a rim. Melt the butter in a large, heavy pot over medium heat. Add nutmeg, cayenne,

and flour. Cook without browning for approximately a minute while whisking continually, or until the mixture starts to boil. Whisk in the wine and milk gradually. Cook for about 2 minutes, whisking continually, until the mixture is smooth, thick, and starting to boil. Bring to a boil. In a small bowl, combine the yolks, salt, and pepper. Instantaneously pour in the yolk mixture and whisk it into the sauce to combine. Stir add 1/4 cup of Parmesan cheese and 1 1/4 bowls of Gruyère cheese (cheeses do not need to melt). Whites should be beaten in a big basin with an electric mixer until firm but not dry. To lighten, fold 1/4 of the whites into a lukewarm soufflé base. The remaining whites are folded in. Place the prepared bowl with the soufflé mixture inside. Add the final 2 tablespoons of Gruyère cheese.

2. Place soufflé in oven and lower temperature to 375°F. For big soufflés, bake for about 40 minutes (or 25 minutes for little soufflés), or until golden and softly set in the centre. Soufflé should be moved to a plate and served right away using oven mitts.

102. BERRY CHIA PUDDING

Active: 5 mins

Total: 8 hrs 5 mins

Servings: 2

Ingredients:

- 1 ¾ bowls blackberries, raspberries and diced mango (fresh or frozen), divided
- 1 bowl of unsweetened almond milk or milk of choice

- ¼ bowl of chia seeds
- 1 tbsp pure maple syrup
- ¾ tsp vanilla remove
- ½ bowl whole-milk plain Greek yoghurt
- ¼ bowl granola

Instructions:

1. Blend or process milk and 1 1/4 bowls of fruit until completely smooth. Mix chia, syrup, and vanilla after scraping into a medium bowl. For at least eight hours & up to three days, cover and chill.
2. Layer each dish of pudding with 1/4 bowl of the remaining fruit, 1/4 bowl of yoghurt, and 2 tbsp granola. Divide the pudding into 2 bowls.

Tips:

Making ahead: Pudding (Step 1) should be refrigerated for up to 3 days.

Nutrition Facts:

Serving Size: about 1 1/3 bowls

Per Serving: 343 calories; protein 13.8g; carbohydrates 39.4g; dietary fibre 14.9g; sugars 17.6g; fat 15.4g; saturated fat 2.8g; cholesterol 8.3mg; vitamin a iu 479.4IU; vitamin c 27mg; folate 59.1mcg; calcium 512.7mg; iron 3.5mg; magnesium 139.6mg; potassium 572.8mg; sodium 125.2mg; added sugar 6g.

Made in the USA
Columbia, SC
14 November 2024

46532765R00083